מדריך לברית מילה ולפדיון הבן

Guide to Ritual Circumcision
and
Redemption
of the First-Born Son

BRITH MILAH
Watercolor by Chaim Gross

מדריך לברית מילה ולפדיון הבן

Guide to Ritual Circumcision
and
Redemption
of the First-Born Son

by
Rabbi Eugene J. Cohen

Ktav Publishing House, Inc.
New York
1984

Library of Congress Cataloging in Publication Data

Cohen, Eugene J. (Eugene Joseph)
   Guide to ritual circumcision and redemption of the
first-born son = [Madrikh li-verit milah ule-fidyon ha-
ben]

   Text in English; liturgy in English and Hebrew.
   Bibliography: p.
   Includes index.
   1. Berit milah. 2. Redemption of the first-born.
I. Title. II. Title: Madrikh li-verit milah ule-fidyon
ha-ben.
BM705.C64   1984   296.4′422   84-5786
ISBN 0-88125-018-X
ISBN 0-88125-023-6 (pbk.)

Manufactured in the United States of America

To
my wife Ada
my mother
and my mother-in-law ז"ל

Contents

vii

PART II—PIDYON HABEN

Contents   xi

Illustrations

Introduction

The Brith Milah Board of New York was founded in 1914 by the Kehillah (Jewish community) of New York City. The Kehillah, an organization that promised unity for the Jews of New York, was soon ravaged by political strife. The only organization established by the Kehillah that continues to function today is the Brith Milah Board. This is because virtually all Jews realize the importance of ritual circumcision and understand that it is a fundamental tenet which merits support.

Questions from all parts of the United States and from many countries of the world have been directed to the board since its inception. We have consulted with eminent rabbis and physicians for answers to questions which do not appear in the literature.

This work is a guide to ritual circumcision and redemption of the first-born son. There are basically two methods of presenting these subjects: (1) the technique of the Responsa literature—stating the question and giving the appropriate answer; and (2) omitting the questions and presenting the answers in a systematic form. The second method was selected because it allows for a more comprehensive presentation.

The material treated in this guide is organized in a forthright and concise manner. Notes have been included to enable the reader to delve more deeply into each detail of the subject. An extensive bibliography provides further assistance. In addition, the guide contains the text of the services for ritual circumcision and the redemption of the first-born son, including a new translation and transliteration. Moreover, a recommendation is presented to solve the vexing problem whereby, while virtually all Jewish boys are circumcised, 80 percent of these children are not circumcised properly. The training of mohelim is also discussed—in the first school of its kind in history; as well as anatomy, technique, and the continuing dispute on routine circumcision.

I pray that this work may add substantially to the understanding and practice of *Brith Milah* and *Pidyon Haben*. May the Lord shower the fullness of His blessings on the people of the covenant.

Acknowledgments

Two categories of acknowledgments are in order: first, to those who have made outstanding contributions to ritual circumcision, and second, to those who have contributed their expertise to this guide.

We are grateful to Rabbi Leo Jung, president of the Brith Milah Boards, for his guidance and leadership.

Dr. Elliot Leiter has earned a lion's share of the credit for the success of the school for *mohelim* and for his responses to the detractors of circumcision. Dr. Arthur I. Eidelman was instrumental in making the inservice workshops for *mohelim* a valuable educational vehicle. They were assisted by physicians, *mohelim*, and rabbis. Rabbi Ephraim Rubin, a certified *mohel*, has wholeheartedly supported all the projects of the board.

Special thanks are due to the executive leaders of the New York Board of Rabbis—Rabbi Harold H. Gordon, of blessed memory, and his successor, Rabbi Paul L. Hait; Rabbi Isaac N. Trainin of the Federation of Jewish Philanthropies of New York; and Rabbi Solomon Schiff, Rabbinical Association of Greater Miami.

Jews from Russia began arriving on our shores in 1971 after decades of the Soviet Union's Iron Curtain policy. Many of the children and young people had not been circumcised, and their parents were very eager to have them brought into the Covenant of Abraham. The youngsters, too, wanted *Brith Milah* in order to be initiated into the Household of Israel. The Brith Milah Board was the only organization in New York City able to provide this service, and it was, of course, delighted to serve our newly arrived brethren. Two years later, the number of new immigrants grew from a trickle into a large wave. Fortunately, volunteer groups and organizations did not let us falter and assisted the board in fulfilling this great *mitzvah*. At this writing, *Brith Milah* has been performed on more than 10,000 Jews from Russia in New York City. We thank the *mohelim*, as well as the cooperating hospitals, urologists, anesthesiologists, and nurses, for their participation. The Federation of Jewish Philanthropies of New York provides partial funding for this sacred cause.

Because only half of the new arrivals remained in New York, other communities were called on to provide similar services. The Brith Milah Board offered guidance and advice, when requested.

Valuable assistance for this guide was received from several specialists, including the late Rabbi Aryeh Kaplan, a prolific Jewish author, who was always ready to help. He read the manuscript and provided important insights. Rabbi David M. Feldman, a renowned scholar, was very helpful. My nephew Mr. Eric Nussbaum and Mrs. Bracha Sachs suggested editorial revisions. My sons, Drs. Burton A. Cohen and Leeber Cohen, and my son-in-law, Dr. Michael A. Goldenhersh, made valuable contributions. Their efforts are sincerely appreciated.

I consulted frequently with my friend Professor David Mirsky, of blessed memory. His untimely death is a source of anguish to his family and friends, and to the community.

Mr. Chaim Gross graciously permitted the republication of his artistic renderings. I am grateful to the curators of the Ferkauf Museum, the International Synagogue at John F. Kennedy International Airport, the Jewish Museum in New York City, and the Israel Museum, Jerusalem, for permission to reprint items from their collections. The librarians of Yeshiva University and the Jewish Theological Seminary of America were very helpful.

The author is neither a *mohel* nor a *Cohen* (priest). *Brith Milah* has been his avocation not his vocation. He is Chief of Chaplains at the Veterans Administration Medical Center, Brooklyn, New York. He is grateful to God for permitting him to complete this labor of love.

Rabbi Eugene J. Cohen, Ph.D.

Part I
BRITH MILAH

CIRCUMCISION CURTAIN

Curtain for the circumcision ceremony. Beige pile;
blue silk; metallic embroidery; stumpwork;
sequins; Hannover or Danzig: 1760. Curtains such
as this one may have been hung above the chair on
which the infant was held during the circumcision
ceremony.

1

The Eternal Covenant

HISTORY

Brith Milah, the covenant of circumcision, was commanded by God to Abraham, the father of the Jewish people, as an eternal bond between Himself and the household of Israel.[1] The Torah states: "I will establish My covenant between Me and you and your children after you, throughout all generations, as an everlasting covenant, to be your God and your children's after you."[2]

The *mitzvah* of *Brith Milah* is unique in that it is sealed in the flesh of the Jew.[3] The Talmud tells us that King David, while in the bathhouse one day, exclaimed, "I am unfortunate because I stand naked, without the opportunity to fulfill any of the commandments." Then he recalled the *Brith Milah,* which was permanently in his flesh, and he became serene.[4]

There has been almost total compliance with this sacred commandment since it was first given to Abraham 3,700 years ago. Only once did our people willingly abstain from observing this *mitzvah*—during the forty years that the young nation was in the wilderness of Sinai, between the time of their redemption from bondage in Egypt and their entry into the Promised Land.

The Talmud explains that the Israelites did not circumcise their children in the desert because of the extreme climate, which could have endangered the children's well-being. Furthermore, the Israelites never knew when they would be told to resume their trek through the wilderness, and conditions on the desert march would not have been safe for newly circumcised infants.[5]

3

There have been other occasions in Jewish history when it was necessary to suspend the *milah* rite. The first such incident was brought about by Jezebel, the daughter of the non-Jewish king of the Sidonians. She became a queen of the Jewish people but was hostile to our religion. Jezebel introduced the idolatrous Baal worship and prohibited the practice of *milah*.[6]

On the other hand, Jews often defied hostile regimes in order to carry out ritual circumcisions, even at the cost of martyrdom. Both the Greeks and the Romans banned *Brith Milah*.[7] They understood correctly that this distinctive rite is the cornerstone of our faith, and that prohibiting *Brith Milah* would be the first step toward eliminating the Jewish people. Stringent edicts were issued against its practice, but Jewish mothers stood up to the mighty conquerors and were prepared to sacrifice their children and themselves rather than forsake *Brith Milah*.

In 1492, after a full century of religious persecution, Spain gave the Jews a final ultimatum—convert to Christianity, leave the country, or be executed. To circumcise one's son was, therefore, to sign one's own death warrant. Even during this difficult period heroic Jews risked death rather than abandon *Brith Milah*.[8]

Such heroism on behalf of ritual circumcision has continued in modern times. We have recently become aware, for instance, of unsung sacrificial incidents wherein Jews incarcerated in Russian jails performed circumcision on themselves without benefit of anesthesia. Such bravery should not go unnoticed.

During the last few years many thousands of Jews liberated from Russia have arrived on our shores. Additional thousands have found a haven in Israel. One of the first requests of these escapees from tyranny was that they and their children be circumcised. The Brith Milah Board of New York, and other organizations throughout the United States, have had the privilege of bringing them into the Covenant of Abraham. Needless to say, the Rabbinate in Israel and its agencies have provided for the circumcision of Jewish arrivals from Russia, when needed.

The Holocaust has been correctly characterized as "The War Against the Jews."[9] I relate just one report among many from this inhuman period in history:

Five years had passed since their marriage, and the couple had been childless. Now, in the very ghetto itself, under Nazi oppression, they were blessed with a son. They lived in Block #3. When the mohel was about to circumcise the infant, the sound of a car stopping outside the building became audible, and from the car Gestapo officials emerged. We were filled with consternation. The mohel's hands trembled. We were all at a loss. What should we do? How could we save the mother and her infant? We trembled. Bravest among us was the mother herself. She turned impatiently to the mohel: Hurry up! Circumcise the child! See, they've come to kill us. Let the child at least die as a Jew."[10]

THE IMPORTANCE OF BRITH MILAH

The Talmud sets forth the primary importance of *Brith Milah*. Rabbi Yehudah the Prince is quoted as saying that *Brith Milah* is more important than any of the other Biblical commandments.[11] In more mystical language, we are told that were it not for the Covenant of Abraham, heaven and earth could not exist.[12]

In codifying Talmudic law, Maimonides observed that circumcision is unlike any other commandment, for the obligation to circumcise continues indefinitely until it is accomplished.[13] That is, if one neglects to eat *matzah* during Passover, nothing can be done to rectify the neglect once the festival has gone by. The same holds true for the observance of the festival of Sukkoth; when the period of obligation passes, the *mitzvah* can no longer be fulfilled. The responsibility for *Brith Milah,* however, remains in force each and every day until it is performed.

Rabbi Joseph B. Soleveitchik explained the significance of *Brith Milah* thus: "It is an eternal covenant which can never be cancelled. The Jewish people and God belong to one existential experience."[14] "The *brith* is the community living in history. Otherwise, man is like a particle of sand floating in tide—coming from nowhere and going nowhere."[15]

In the words of another contemporary rabbi: "To some degree, circumcision restored Abraham and his descendants to the status of Adam before his sin. It was because they were circumcised that

Abraham's descendants were able to be the recipients of the Torah. Thus, it was through the commandment of circumcision that the purpose of creation could be fulfilled."[16]

RESPONSIBILITY

The obligation to circumcise lies with the father of a newborn boy.[17] Should he be unable or unwilling, the obligation rests with the mother.[18] When neither father nor mother makes the necessary arrangements, the responsibility devolves upon the rabbinic court (*Beth Din*) of the community.[19] Finally, if no one assumes the task of circumcising the child, the responsibility falls on every member of the Jewish community.[20]

LOCALE FOR THE BRITH MILAH

The locale for the performance of *Brith Milah* has changed a number of times in the course of history. When infants were born at home, the *brith* was usually conducted in the synagogue,[21] in order to add beauty and sanctity to the *mitzvah.*[22] When hospital delivery became more common, the hospital became the site of the circumcision, and many hospitals designated a Brith Milah Room for this purpose. Since World War II, however, mothers and babies have customarily been discharged from the hospital prior to the eighth day. Military physicians had determined that it was perfectly safe for mother and child to leave the hospital earlier, and when the physicians returned to civilian life they continued to so advise.

This new development inadvertently created a problem for the proper performance of *Brith Milah*. Parents are frequently reluctant to have the *brith* at home. The mother is not "up to" having a party in her home shortly after giving birth. This "party" refers to the tradition of having a meal after the rite of circumcision (*Seudath Mitzvah*). Another reason offered is that the apartment is too small for a large gathering. In Chapter 8, it will be shown that neither the meal nor the quorum of ten men is required, though both are desirable. What is essential is that the baby be circumcised by a *mohel* on the eighth day.

All too often, parents allow the circumcision to take place in the hospital before the eighth day and in a manner that is bereft of religious significance. What should and could have been a *Brith Milah* is transformed into a surgical procedure. Furthermore, when circumcision takes place before the eighth day, it is invalid and requires a corrective procedure known as *hatafath dam brith,* the extraction of a drop of blood, after the child has healed from the circumcision. This subject will be discussed in greater detail in Chapter 2.

It is advisable to return to the practice of having the *Brith Milah* in the synagogue. In this way the *brith* and the *Seudath Mitzvah* could take place without inconvenience to the parents, amidst beauty and holiness.

NAMING OF THE CHILD

The naming of a boy takes place at the *Brith Milah,* while a girl is named in the synagogue on a day when the Torah is read.[23] There is no time limit for the naming of a girl, but it is customarily done as soon as it is feasible. One rabbinic authority recommends that the naming of a baby girl take place when the mother is well enough to attend services in the synagogue, to enable her to be present when the child is named and to hear the prayer offered for the speedy and complete recovery of mother and child.[24]

Ashkenazim, as a rule, do not name a child after a living person, but Sephardim consider it propitious to do so. Our sages recommend that the name given to a child, whether boy or girl, be chosen with care, so that the child will have a proper model to emulate.[25]

It is permissible to use only part of the name, or even only the first consonant. Parents may want to name a boy after a deceased female relative. In such a case an appropriate masculine name with the same first consonant as the female relative's name is given. When this is done, the parents' next child should not be named after the same individual.

There are authoritative opinions that when a child requires a prolonged delay until he is circumcised, that the naming may take place prior to the *brith*. The prevailing custom is to wait with the naming until the *brith*.[26]

2

The Date of the Circumcision

"You will circumcise the flesh of your foreskin, and this will be a sign of the covenant between Me and you."[1] As this Biblical verse demonstrates, circumcision is testimony to the relationship between God and the Jewish people. It is not merely a surgical procedure, and should not be treated as one. It must be performed in accordance with the laws and customs prescribed by the Torah and our sages.

THE EIGHTH DAY

The circumcision must be performed on the eighth day during the daylight hours. "He that is eight days old shall be circumcised . . ."[2] A circumcision that takes place before the eighth day or during the night is invalid, and in such cases a drop of blood (*hatafath dam brith*) must be drawn, once the original circumcision has healed, to validate the circumcision.[3]

The eighth day is so essential to the proper performance of *Brith Milah* that it supersedes the Sabbath and holy days. The *mohel* may do all that the circumcision requires on the Sabbath.[4] The instruments and all the needed equipment, however, should be in readiness before the Sabbath at the location where the *brith* will take place.[5]

One scholar suggests that *Brith Milah* supersedes the Sabbath because the results remain permanently on the body of the Jew, whereas the Sabbath concludes on Saturday night.[6] Another

9

scholar states that we may compare the *Brith Milah* to the sacrificial service in the Temple, where the *Cohen* was authorized to perform his sacred task on the Sabbath even though it included transgressions of the Sabbath laws.[7] The *mohel,* like the *Cohen* of old, must fulfill his sacred obligations even when they violate the Sabbath. This refers, of course, only to the actual act of circumcision. Everything possible must be done prior to the Sabbath. Since the actual *Brith Milah,* however, may not be performed ahead of time, it is permitted on the Sabbath.[7]

We are familiar with the fact that when one day of Rosh Hashanah is on a Sabbath, we refrain from sounding the *shofar* that day. Likewise, when Sukkoth is on a Sabbath, we do not wave the *lulav* until the following day. We abstain from these *mitzvoth* because of the possibility that a person may carry the *shofar* or the *lulav* from a private domain, his home, to a public domain, the street, which is forbidden on the Sabbath.[8]

Our sages explained why the concern that an object related to the *mitzvah* might be "carried" on the Sabbath does not apply to *Brith Milah.*[9] Circumcision is different because only those who are specially trained may undertake this *mitzvah.* While it is true that every Jew is permitted to perform *Brith Milah,* an individual does not actually *become* a *mohel* until he is properly trained and authorized.[10] Consequently, since *mohelim* are thoroughly trained, we are confident that a *mohel* will not unintentionally carry from one domain to another.

It is very unusual for a child to require medical care following *Brith Milah.* Should this be necessary, however, the laws of the Sabbath are put aside and everything necessary is done to bring the child to a speedy recovery.[11]

In Chapter 1 the return to the custom of having the *Brith Milah* in the synagogue was recommended. But what if the correct date for the *brith* is on a Sabbath in a community that does not have an *eruv,* the fusing of the public and private domains? Our sages differ as to whether a non-Jew may carry the baby from the home into the public domain.[12] Since there is no definitive ruling, it is best in this instance to have the *brith* at home, unless there is an overriding reason for not doing so.

It is vital that the laws of the Sabbath not be transgressed in the locale where the *brith* takes place. There are rabbinic opinions that in instances where this will occur, it is best to postpone the *brith* to the following day. A leading authority, however, maintains that having the *brith* on the eighth day cannot be abrogated even for so serious a reason.[13]

THE HEALTH OF THE CHILD

The health of the child is the factor that determines whether the *Brith Milah* can take place on the eighth day. Maimonides states the ruling very simply: "It is forbidden to circumcise a child who has any illness, because life-threatening problems postpone everything. It is possible to circumcise on a later date, but it is impossible to restore a life."[14]

There are two categories of sick children. If the child has a systemic disease (*choleh b'khol gufo*), we are required to wait seven days after the child is well before having the *brith*. If it is not a systemic disease, but a minor problem, the *brith* may be performed as soon as the child is well.[15] According to many authorities, it is a law pronounced by Moses at Sinai (*halakhah l'Moshe m'Sinai*) that a sick child has his prescribed time for circumcision (*z'man milah*) suspended and a new time occurs.[16]

It is essential that medical clearance be obtained from the physician prior to planning the *Brith Milah*. The parent or the *mohel* may not assume that because delivery took place in a hospital, this clearance was given prior to the baby's discharge. There are occasions when the pediatric resident does not examine the baby before discharge.[17] The parents and the *mohel* must ascertain whether the baby is medically well, and this may only be determined by a physician.

There are instances where medical clearance is given but the *mohel* refuses to perform the *brith*, based on religious laws that declare the child is not ready for circumcision. The following principle is applied in evaluating rabbinic and medical decisions:

When the sages maintain that a tradition was handed down from

Sinai, we do not heed the physicians. When, however, the rabbis refer to a medical problem and say that something is dangerous, this need not be accepted, because this may change with time. The rabbis, furthermore, may have received this information from physicians, which may no longer be scientific fact. We obey the physicians when they cite principles of medicine, but when they declare this to be an exceptional case, we must consider and evaluate most carefully.[18]

3

The Mohel

It is the obligation of the father to circumcise his son. This is based on the verse "And Abraham circumcised his son Isaac."[1] In most instances the father is not trained in *milah*. Therefore, he delegates his responsibility to the *mohel*.

The definition of *mohel* is "ritual circumciser," and the plural form is *mohelim*. Since the beginning of Jewish history there has been a need for *mohelim* to perform the sacred rite. The Talmud states that a scholar may not reside in a community that does not have a *mohel*.[2]

TRAINING OF THE MOHEL

The record of *mohelim* has been superb. This glorious achievement is due to the intensive training that the *mohel* receives prior to acquiring the status of certified *mohel*. Instruction is by the time-honored preceptor method. The preceptor, or teacher, imparts his knowledge and experience to the student. The training of a *mohel* has only one criterion—excellence. The course of training does not have a prescribed duration—each candidate advances at his own pace.

The instruction of the student is in three areas: (1) science, including anatomy, hematology, asepsis, physiology, microbiology

13

and pathology; (2) the techniques of sterilization and the preoperative, operative, and postoperative phases of circumcision; and (3) Jewish laws and traditions that apply to *Brith Milah,* including Talmudic literature, Codes, Responsa, and at least one *milah* textbook.

Clinical training begins with student observation of the preceptor performing circumcisions. After every *Brith Milah* the preceptor explains exactly what he did in order to enable the student to observe more intelligently. The preceptor decides when the student may do a part of *Brith Milah.* When this segment is done perfectly, the student is permitted to do an additional phase. This procedure continues until the candidate is able to perform a complete *Brith Milah.* The student then continues to circumcise many children under the supervision of the preceptor.

When the teacher is convinced that the candidate is qualified for certification, he recommends him to the local Brith Milah Board, which consists of rabbis, *mohelim,* and physicians, who examine the candidate for his knowledge, piety, and expertise.[3] This millennia-old procedure of training and certifying has brought honor and respect to the profession of *mohel.*

Hospitals, with very rare exceptions, accept this accreditation and appoint the *mohel* to the hospital staff. The *mohel* serves as a member of the health team and works harmoniously with the doctors, nurses, and other health personnel.

The reader will now appreciate why the training of a *mohel* has no bounds in time. There are many factors to be considered. The House of Israel has been blessed with excellent *mohelim* during the past thirty-seven centuries because of the intensive training that each *mohel* receives.

The Brith Milah Board of New York, in its quest to maintain the high standards of *mohelim,* opened the first school in Jewish history to teach ritual circumcision. The best experiences of the past and the present were incorporated in the school. The institution was called the Brith Milah School Conducted at The Mount Sinai Hospital, and it admitted its first class in March 1968. Several other hospitals cooperated with this project, including

Beth Israel Medical Center, Jewish Memorial Hospital, Brookdale Medical Center, Long Island Jewish Medical Center, and the Albert Einstein Hospital of Yeshiva University.

In organizing the school we had the experience of the preceptor method. There were didactic lectures in science and Jewish law. Urologists, hematologists, pediatricians, obstetricians, Talmudists, and ethicists generously shared their knowledge and expertise with the students. Certified *mohelim* who had previously prepared candidates by the preceptor method provided clinical training. The school was funded by the Federation of Jewish Philanthropies of New York with grants to the New York Board of Rabbis. The school stopped functioning temporarily when sufficient *mohelim* had been graduated to serve the needs of the community.

The achievement of certification is not the end of the *mohel*'s learning experience, but only the beginning. The *mohel* constantly updates his knowledge by continuing to study scientific and religious literature, consulting with colleagues, and participating in inservice training.

In communities blessed with more than one *mohel,* parents should consult their rabbi in order to choose the best-qualified mohel.[4]

A concluding word about the *mohel*'s role and the father's duty. When the father delegates the *mohel* to perform the *Brith Milah* rite, he has not completed his obligation. He and the *mohel* must have the proper intention (*kavanah*) when the *brith* takes place. Both should bear in mind that they are fulfilling the command of God.[5] The *mohel,* in particular, should recall the thought expressed by one rabbi, that in performing this rite, it is as though he is observing *all* of the 613 commandments.[6]

PHYSICIAN AS MOHEL

A physician may serve as a *mohel,*[7] but his medical training while a valuable asset, does not replace religious knowledge and observance. The fact that one is a physician does not automatically qualify him to be a *mohel.* Rabbis have objected to physicians serving as *mohelim* because this might open the door to physicians who were not observant Jews.[8] When a physician serves as a *mohel* in a community where there is a *mohel,* he is competing with the *mohel,* who is dependent on his holy work for a livelihood.

WHERE THERE IS NO MOHEL

What should parents do when they reside in an area where there is no *mohel?* This problem has often faced American military personnel stationed in the Pacific. May one opt for a person who is not religiously qualified to perform *Brith Milah?* Our sages have dealt with this question since Talmudic times.

Two considerations must be weighed in determining the law in such a case. First, the Torah commands, "And you shall keep My Covenant" (Genesis 17:9). This verse teaches that anyone who does not observe Judaism is disqualified from performing *Brith Milah.* Thus a non-Jew or a disbelieving Jew is not permitted to be a *mohel.* But there is a second consideration: that the baby must be circumcised. Most rabbinic authorities have ruled that it is preferable to leave the child uncircumcised rather than have the circumcision performed by one who is disqualified (*posul*).[9]

The Brith Milah Board of America counsels such families to consider traveling to the nearest place where there is a *mohel,* or to arrange for the *mohel* to travel to them. Today's jet travel has helped resolve problems that were insurmountable in the past.

4

Postponement of the Brith Milah

It was noted in Chapter 2 that in instances where the child is not well, we are forbidden to perform the *brith* until he is restored to good health. There are both illnesses and anomalies that can result in the postponing of circumcision. The laws of the Torah are meant to be lived by—not, God forbid, to endanger anyone. Thus, in all such cases, we wait until the physician says that the baby is well. Then we can decide when the *brith* will take place.[1]

THE JAUNDICED INFANT

When a baby's skin has a yellow color, a blood test is necessary to determine whether he has a high bilirubin. The yellow color itself poses no problem, but it may be due to a high bilirubin, a pigment in the blood. The bilirubin can enter the brain of the child and cause a form of cerebral palsy and brain damage known as kernicterus. Since it is extremely difficult to know how high the bilirubin is by merely looking at the baby, it must be measured chemically with a blood test.

Frequently, physicians will have the mother stop breastfeeding to lower the bilirubin. The rabbis, however, rule that the baby is not to be denied this nourishment unless it is required for medical reasons. We simply delay the *brith*. "Should the jaundice persist, we must wait seven days, beginning the count when the child is well."[2]

As a noted authority has explained, the normal term baby's bilirubin will go up during the first 48–72 hours, level off and start to come down. He should have no major rise in bilirubin after the 4th or 5th day of life. The bilirubin of the premature baby without any disease will continue to rise beyond the 4th day and peak as late as one week. It takes longer for his liver to mature.[3]

NOLAD MAHUL

The literal translation of *nolad mahul* is "one who is born circumcised." In such cases, the corona is perfectly clear without a prepuce or mucous membrane. Since the child has no prepuce, he cannot be circumcised. But does he require the drawing of a drop of blood as a sign of the covenant? And if this is necessary, may the drawing of the drop of blood take place on the Sabbath, when this is the baby's eighth day of life? Our sages have deliberated these two questions since the time of the Talmud.[4]

During the present century, the question of a child born without a prepuce has been academic. There have been no recorded cases of such an event.[5] When a child appears to have been born circumcised, he actually has a prepuce but it is pressed against the membrum and cannot be distinguished. This is called an *orlah kh'vusha*.

In such cases, the *mohel* examines the child carefully. Should the *mohel* be unable to find a rudimentary prepuce, the circumcision is delayed until the child becomes older and more developed. If, however, a small amount of prepuce is found, the circumcision may be performed. Should the infant's eighth day be a Sabbath or a holiday, the *brith* is delayed until after the Sabbath or holiday. During the *brith,* more of the prepuce may become visible. This is usually peeled off.

If it is substantiated when the child has grown older that he has no prepuce or mucous membrane, then all that need be done is to extract a drop of blood, and this is his circumcision. In view of the fact that this will occur long after the eighth day, the drop of blood may not be drawn on a Sabbath or a holiday.

HYPOSPADIAS, CHORDEE, EPISPADIUS, AND TUMTUM

The definition of hypospadius is that the orifice or the meatal opening is lower than normal, located on the underside of the penis. The term comes from the Greek *hypo,* meaning "under," and *spadon,* meaning "to tear off." A hypospadius is a torn-off urethra that falls short of the normal position and does not reach the end of the penis. There are varying degrees in the position of the opening. It may be mid-penile, penoscrotal, coronal, or mid-glanular.

The *mohel* is trained to recognize abnormalities of the penis. It is still wise, though, to obtain a physician's professional opinion as to whether or not circumcision may take place. There are occasions where reconstruction will be necessary and a portion of the foreskin will be needed. The foreskin may be required because it is the only skin other than the palms of the hands and soles of the feet that does not have hair. This is especially true if the child also has chordee, or curvature of the penis.

When reconstruction is necessary, the circumcision is delayed until the time of the surgery. The *mohel* goes into the operating room with the physician, says the blessing for *Brith Milah,* and makes an incision. The surgeon follows the *mohel* with the repair. This malformation occurs once in 130 male children.[6]

There are occasions where a child is diagnosed as having severe hypospadius with chordee when he actually is a true hermaphrodite with both ovarian and testicular tissues.[7] Physicians can transform this person into a male or a female. The halakhic determination as to whether the child is to be circumcised is decided by the chromosome. If the child has a "Y" chromosome, he is a male. A "Y" chromosome means testes, and testes signify a male. It does not matter whether the testes are descended or undescended.[8]

Epispadias is a very rare anomaly. This term, too, is from the Greek. *Epi* means "upon," *spadon* is "to tear." This is a malformation in which the urethra opens on the dorsum, or upper part, of the penis.

Tumtum is yet another anomaly where a caul, or heavy skin, covers the scrotal area and there is no sign of external genitalia. The Talmud did not recommend removing the caul of a *tumtum,* because the child might become infected. Should the caul be removed, the sex of the child can be easily determined.[9]

CAESAREAN SECTION

A child who was delivered by Caesarean, or abdominal, section is circumcised on the eighth day. However, if the eighth day is a Sabbath or a holiday, the *brith* is postponed till after the Sabbath or holiday. The rabbis explain that the Sabbath is superseded by *Brith Milah* only in instances where the mother becomes ritually unclean (*t'mai'ah*) because of delivery.[10]

BAIN HASHEMASHOTH

The term *bain hashemashoth* refers to twilight. This is the point in time which lies between day and night but which cannot be precisely ascribed to either. When a child is born during twilight, is his first day of life the one ending or the one about to begin? Determining the correct day is important for deciding when the *brith* will take place.[11]

Let us say that a baby is born on Friday at twilight. If twilight belongs to the previous day, then the day of the *brith* would be Friday. If twilight belongs to the following day, then the *brith* would take place on the Sabbath. But since we cannot have a doubtful *brith* on the Sabbath, the *brith* would be postponed to Sunday. Should Sunday and Monday be a Jewish holiday, the *brith* must be delayed to Tuesday. A *brith* only supersedes the Sabbath and holidays when it falls on the eighth day. When the date of birth is in doubt, we postpone the *brith* to the succeeding weekday.[12]

The generally accepted custom in New York City is that the day ends with the astronomical sunset (*sh'kiah*). The next forty-five minutes comprise *bain hashemashoth,* or twilight, the period that is in doubt, and immediately thereafter night begins.[13]

Candle-lighting time has no bearing on determining the day the child was born. Thus, even if the Sabbath or festival candles were already lit when the child was born, since it is still day, the *brith* should take place the following Friday or the day before the festival. The same holds true with regard to the evening prayers (*Maariv* service). Saying these prayers before sunset does not affect the date of the *brith*.[14]

The computation of sunset, twilight, and night refers to New York City and other communities in the same latitude. Those who reside in communities that are farther north or south should consult Leo Levi's *Jewish Chrononomy* for the time of sunset and the duration of twilight in their areas.[15]

There are occasions when a baby is born precisely at sunset. The Mishnah states: "When the child is born in the normal manner, it is deemed born when the greater part of its head issued forth. And what is meant by the 'greater part of its head'? As soon as the forehead emerges."[16] A leading authority wrote that the word "forehead" in the Mishnah refers to the *major* part of the forehead.[17]

The time of birth is calculated differently by *Halakhah* than by the obstetrician. *Halakhah* considers birth to have taken place when the major part of the forehead has come forth from the mother's body; the physician calculates birth from the time when the entire body has been expelled or extracted. The difference between these two systems may vary from seconds to a minute or more. It is, therefore, necessary to ask the obstetrician how much time elapsed after the major part of the forehead came out of the uterus.[18]

The above applies only when the child is delivered in the "normal" manner. When the child is delivered by Caesarean section, the halakhic time will be identical with the obstetrician's recorded time.

CLASSIFICATION OF THE NEWBORN BY BIRTH WEIGHT AND GESTATIONAL AGE

Until the 1960s, a premature infant was defined as a newborn who weighed less than 5 pounds 8 ounces (2500 grams). Dr. Lubchenco, a pathologist from Denver, suggested another way of measuring the child—the gestational age. Children born at less than thirty-eight weeks are pre-term, or premature. Those born between thirty-eight and forty-two weeks are of normal gestation. Infants born after forty-two weeks gestation are post-term.[19] The pediatrician has criteria to determine that an infant is premature even if it weighs more than 5½ pounds. Conversely a child who weighs less than 5½ pounds may be mature.[20]

There are many other questions that must be answered before a *brith* may be performed. Were there problems in pregnancy, labor, or delivery? The medical history of the parents should be checked to make certain that there are no other problems.

"Babies are now sent home from the premature nurseries at 4 pounds 11 ounces depending upon evaluation of their physiologic stability." Physicians maintain that when a child is discharged from the hospital he is ready for *Brith Milah.*[21]

Medical clearance should be obtained prior to performing *Brith Milah.* Should the doctor advise a postponement of the *brith,* this has the validity of a halakhic decision.

STILLBORN AND NONVIABLE INFANTS

In the case of a stillborn, the prepuce is removed. The same is true of an infant who dies before the eighth day and of a child who lived longer than eight days but was too weak to be circumcised. No blessings are recited because there is no obligation for *Brith Milah* in such a tragedy. The baby is given a name so that he will be included in the Resurrection of the Dead.[22] These customs pertain only when the baby has the Talmud's anatomical signs for a mature baby—developed fingernails and hair. These practices are a tradition taught by the Gaonim.

HEMOPHILIA

Hemophelia is defined as "hereditary hemorrhagic diathesis due to deficiency of coagulation Factor VIII."[23] "Credit for the first delineation of the disease must be given to a U.S. physician, John C. Otto, who described in 1803 ' . . . an hemorrhagic disposition existing in certain families.'" Only males are subject to this affliction. Females are exempt, but they are capable of transmitting it to their male children.[24]

The Mishnah (completed 188 C.E.) was probably the first work to record the results of this malady.[25] The Talmud (redacted 505 C.E.) cites additional cases.[26] The rabbis knew by observation that only males were endangered. They ruled that *Brith Milah* was prohibited for sons born to families with a history of hemophilia.[27] This prohibition is valid even when physicians can reduce the risk.[28]

Factor XI, a form of hemophilia, was first reported in 1953. Most cases occur in Jewish children.[29] A child with Factor XI may be circumcised when the physician approves.

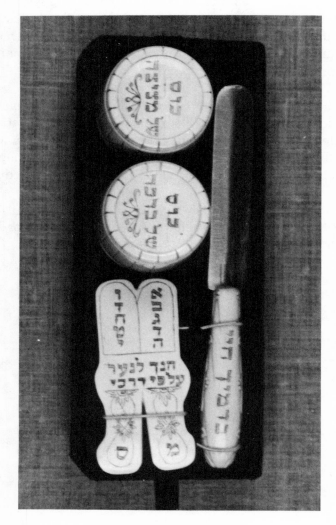

CIRCUMCISION SET
Ivory circumcision set, date unknown.

*Courtesy of the Sol Rozman Collection
at the Ferkauf Museum, International Synagogue,
John F. Kennedy International Airport, New York.
Photo by Dr. Michael Goldenhersh*

5

Determining the Religion of the Child

A *mohel* may perform a *brith* only as a religious rite, on a Jew.[1] Since converting to Judaism is a religious act, a *mohel* may participate in the circumcision.[2] The subject of conversion to Judaism will be discussed in the next chapter.

WHEN ONLY ONE PARENT IS JEWISH

A Jew, by definition, is a person who was born to Jewish parents. In instances where only one parent is Jewish, the religion of the child is determined by that of the mother. Thus, if the mother is Jewish, the child is Jewish. If the mother is not Jewish, the child is not Jewish.[3]

A mother who converts to Judaism is regarded as a Jewess in every respect. Thus, her child's religion is based on whether the child was born before or after the conversion. If the child was born after the conversion, he is, of course, Jewish, because he was born to a Jewish mother. The child is Jewish even if the conversion of the mother took place during pregnancy.[4]

ADOPTION

The regulations are the same with regard to an adopted child. When the natural parents are Jewish, the child is Jewish. Should only one parent be Jewish, the child's religion is dependent on the natural mother. Should the natural mother be non-Jewish, the child needs to be converted, and the first step, in the case of a boy, is *Brith Milah*. The adopting parents assume the responsibility of circumcising the child along with the many other obligations. The circumcision is followed by immersing the child in a ritual bath (*mikvah*) in the presence of a Rabbinic Court (*Beth Din*).[5]

It should be noted that there is a sparsity of Jewish legislation on the adoption of children. Rabbi Immanuel Jakobovits made the following observations to explain the lack of rabbinic law:

> Adoption in the strictly legal sense as understood in Western society does not really exist in Jewish law. Modern legislation in this sphere is founded on Roman law which invested fathers with ownership rights over their children, and the courts with powers to transfer these rights. Jewish law confers no such rights, nor does it empower the courts to establish any legal facts. On the contrary, the facts determine the law, and the courts merely supervise and regulate personal relations into which the parties have entered by their own action. Just as marriages and divorces are executed or granted solely by the parties to them, with rabbis or religious courts acting to ensure that such acts are lawfully performed, so do legal adoptions in Jewish view merely represent obligations which the parties involved have agreed to assume. But no court can create the full equivalent of natural family relations, or replace them. No legal act can supersede or annul the inalienable duties and privileges deriving from the natural bonds between parents and children.[6]

Rabbi Jakobovits explains further that there was no need to regulate the private care of homeless children, because there were none, or so few that halakhic decisions were not needed. He attributes this to

> the rigid standards of Jewish home life, the strong sense of family relations, the highly developed social conscience for the welfare of orphans as a communal responsibility, and the extremely rare incidence of Jewish children born out of wedlock. Only with the apparently growing rate of infertility in modern times, have Jewish adoptions become fairly common, though the demand exceeds the supply.

The term in Hebrew for the adoption of children is *emutz y'ladim*. This is a relatively new expression; it does not appear in Talmudic literature. There is, however, an allusion to adoption in the words: "Anyone who rears an orphaned boy or girl in his home is considered by Scripture as though he had given birth to them."[7] One commentary interprets this passage as including the rearing of any child, not exclusively orphans.[8]

These texts approximate what we know as adoption. In the State of Israel, adoption is governed by the Adoption of Children Law, 5720/1960, which empowers the district rabbinical court, with the consent of all the parties concerned, to grant an adoption order.

An adopted child is called to the Torah as the son of the adoptive father. He does not, however, receive the title of *Cohen* or *Levi* unless his natural father was a *Cohen* or a *Levi*.[9]

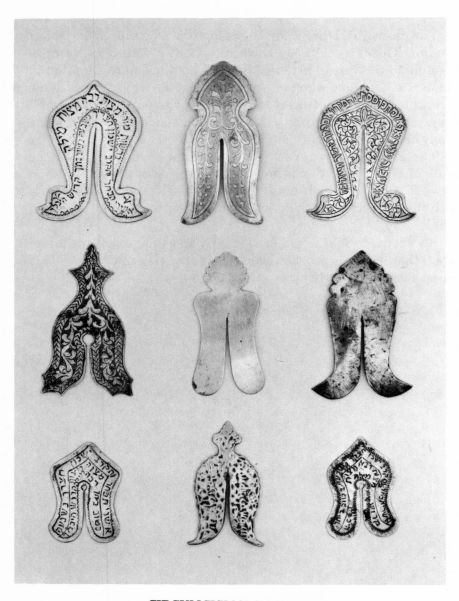

CIRCUMCISION SHIELDS
Circumcision protective shields dating from the Eighteenth Century,
representing Iran, Central and Eastern Europe.

6

Fast-Days and Periods of Mourning

FAST-DAYS

The blessing on the wine is said at a *Brith Milah* which takes place on a fast-day. Young children may drink the wine since they are not required to fast.[1] On Yom Kippur, however, the circumcised infant is given a dab of the gauze dipped in wine. This is in addition to the taste of wine that the baby receives when we chant "live by your blood" (*b'domayikh cha'yi*). When the mother is free from the obligation of fasting on Yom Kippur because of weakness, she may drink from the goblet of wine.[2]

When a *brith* takes place on Tisha B'Av, it is performed at the conclusion of the morning service. The parents, grandparents, *mohel,* and *sandek* are permitted to don their Sabbath clothing in honor of the joyous occasion. After the *brith,* they should change to their weekly attire.[3] The meal (*Seudath Mitzvah*) takes place after sunset.

From Rosh Chodesh Av until the eve of Tisha B'Av, the custom of refraining from eating meat dishes is waived in honor of the *brith.*[4]

Fast-days which occur on the Sabbath are postponed to Sunday, because we may not fast on the Sabbath, with two exceptions. Yom Kippur is never delayed; when it takes place on the Sabbath, we observe Yom Kippur on the Sabbath. The second exception is the Fast of Esther, which is observed on the day before Purim. We cannot postpone the fast to Sunday, for that day is

Purim, and fasting would change the nature of the day, which is supposed to be one of merriment. Consequently, the Fast of Esther is observed on the preceding Thursday.[5]

When a fast-day is postponed, everyone observes the fast, including the immediate participants.[6] However, when the Fast of Esther is brought forward to Thursday, all persons present at the *Brith Milah* may partake of the (*Seudath Mitzvah*), and they fulfill their obligation to fast on the next day, Friday.[7]

Tachanun (elegies and supplications) are omitted on a day when there is a *Brith Milah,* even if it is a fast-day.[8]

TIMES OF MOURNING

There are different periods of mourning. The first is when one is an *onen*—the time following the death but before the deceased has been brought to his or her final resting place. An *onen* is exempt from observing all precepts. Should the father of the baby be an *onen,* he may circumcise his son in the synagogue after the conclusion of the Morning Services, but he does not recite the customary blessings at the *brith.* The blessings are said by the *sandek.*[9]

When it is possible to inter the deceased before the *brith,* the father is no longer in the category of *onen,* and thus he may say the blessings.

When a *mohel* who is to circumcise an infant becomes an *onen,* he may circumcise if there is no other *mohel* available or if the parents want only him to perform the *brith* on their child. But he must inter his deceased relative before performing the *brith.*[10]

The next periods of mourning are the first three days and the balance of the *shiva,* the seven-day mourning period. During both of these periods, the father is permitted to attend services in the synagogue when the *Brith Milah* is scheduled to take place there. If, however, the *Brith Milah* is at home, then both the service and the *brith* are conducted at the home. A *Seudath Mitzvah* is permitted under such circumstances, and the mourner may wear festive clothing for the holy occasion.[11]

The next mourning period is *sh'loshim,* the first thirty days of mourning. A father who is in mourning is permitted to have his hair cut in addition to the above.[12]

During the year of mourning, a mourner who is neither the parent nor the *mohel* customarily refrains from attending the *Seudath Mitzvah*.[13]

During the time that we count the *Omer*, the father, the *mohel*, and the *sandek* are permitted to have their hair cut in honor of the *Brith Milah*.[14]

7

The Convert to Judaism

There are three requirements for the man who wants to become a Jew: (1) acceptance of the "yoke of the commandments," (2) circumcision, and (3) immersion in the ritual bath (*mikvah*), after the circumcision site is healed.[1] If a convert was circumcised previously, a drop of blood must be extracted to fulfill the obligation of *Brith Milah*.

The conversion of an individual to Judaism is essentially the same process by which our forefathers "were accepted like proselytes into their new faith. Immediately after this, the Israelites declared, 'We will do and we will obey' (Exodus 24:7). Whenever a gentile converts to Judaism, he essentially duplicates this oath and covenant."[2]

A person who wants to convert to Judaism is apprised of the difficulties he will face upon conversion. The Talmud suggests that the candidate be asked: "Why do you want to become a proselyte? Do you not know that the Jewish people are persecuted and oppressed?"

There are religious obligations that the proselyte must be willing to accept. He is told that many things that were permissible to him will become forbidden when he becomes a Jew. He must accept the unity of God. The Talmud states that, should the candidate reply that he is aware of the problems and the added responsibilities and accepts them, he is given instruction in some of the major and minor commandments, as well as the rewards for fulfilling them and the punishments for transgression.[3]

33

In practice, however, the minimal requirements of the *Hala-khah* are increased so that the candidate will be more knowledge-able. The convert is generally taught to read Hebrew so that he can pray like other Jews in the synagogue and at home. He is taught Jewish history, customs, and ceremonies. The added instruction impresses upon the proselyte that he is a Jew in fact as well as in name.

When it is affirmed that a male candidate for conversion is intent on becoming a Jew, the second step—*Brith Milah*—is taken. The technique of circumcising an adult is different from the one performed on an infant of eight days. The adult is circumcised in an operating room with the customary precautions. The surgical team scrubs as they would for any other operation. The *mohel* makes the first and last incisions. The major part of the *Brith Milah* is performed by a urologist. There are some *mohelim* who are trained to do this type of circumcision by using the same tech-nique as with an infant. Here too, physicians are needed to admin-ister anesthesia and suturing.

The blessings are offered with an emendation in consonance with the circumstances.[4] At the conclusion of the circumcision, the proselyte is given his Jewish name and is called "the son of Abra-ham, our father."[5]

The third and final step takes place when the circumcision site has healed. The convert immerses himself in a ritual bath (*mikvah*). Immediately prior to the immersion he is once again reminded of the "yoke of the commandments" and is asked whether he accepts them. When he affirms that he is ready and willing to abide by all the requirements, the rabbinic court (*Beth Din*) instructs him to submerge in the ritual bath. When he ascends from the ritual bath, he covers himself with a robe and recites the blessing *al haTvilah*.[6]

Each of the three steps mentioned above is to be done in the presence of a rabbinic court. The three requirements are valid only when they are accomplished during the daylight hours on any day except the Sabbath and/or a holiday.[7]

If a couple converts to Judaism together with their minor children, the latter may revoke the act when they attain the age of majority.[8]

The conversion of a woman is similar to that of a man, except that only two steps are needed: (1) acceptance of the "yoke of the commandments," and (2) ablution in a ritual bath. In the case of a woman, the rabbinic court hears her recite the blessing behind partially closed doors.

There are authorities who maintain that after the candidate has completed the necessary requirements and has become a righteous proselyte (*ger tzedek*), a *Seudath Mitzvah* should be enjoyed. This is based on the text, "And Aaron and all the elders of Israel ate bread with Moses' father-in-law before God."[9]

ELIJAH'S CHAIR
Chair of Elijah (for circumcision). Dermbach, Thuringia, Germany,
1768. Wood, carved and painted.

8

Explanatory Notes on Brith Milah

Throughout Jewish history, many customs have been observed in honor of *Brith Milah.* Some have survived the centuries while others have been altered or discontinued. The rabbis state that *minhag Yisrael k'din hu,* "a Jewish custom has the force of law." For unknown reasons some customs continue while others disappear. Since our people were dispersed in many lands, there are customs indigenous to some countries and not others.

CUSTOMS PRIOR TO CIRCUMCISION

The Talmud mentions two observances, *Yeshua Haben* and *Shavua Haben.*[1] *Yeshua Haben* alludes to the freeing of the infant from the womb of the mother.[2] This custom has been retained with modifications. It is observed on the Friday night before the *Brith Milah.*[3] Family, friends, and neighbors visit the home of the newborn child after completing their Sabbath meal. Sabbath hymns are sung, and it is appropriate that a Torah message be presented. Light refreshments are served so that the gathering may be a *Seudath Mitzvah.* The name of the observance has been changed to *Ben Zakhor,* or "the child of remembrance." This is a play on the tradition that the infant was taught the entire Torah in his mother's womb, but that just before he enters the world an angel touches his lip, so that his Torah knowledge is forgotten.[4] The rabbis taught that the education of a child begins long before birth. Consequently, proper preparations are to be made before giving birth to a child; and the training continues for many years. This celebration is also known as *Shalom Zakhor,* "the welcoming of the male child."

There was a custom to bring schoolchildren to the infant's home every evening prior to the *Brith Milah* to recite the *Sh'ma* and Psalm 128. The custom was discontinued when delivery took place in a hospital rather than at home. The custom is still observed in some quarters.

There are sages who maintain that this Sabbath gathering is based on a Midrash.[5]

> Rabbi Joshua of Siknin in the name of Rabbi Levi said: "It is similar to a decree issued by a king that visitors shall not see him until they have paid their respects to his lady. In the same way the Holy One, Blessed be He, said: 'You shall not bring an offering unto Me until a Sabbath day has passed over it,' and there cannot be seven continuous days without a Sabbath, nor can there be a circumcision without the lapse of a Sabbath."

In the opinion of one commentary, "the week of the son" (*Shavua Haben*) refers to *Brith Milah;* since a week has passed, the following day is the time for the circumcision.[6]

Nachmanides observed that there is a forgotten festivity—the celebration of the birth of a girl (*Shavua Habath*).[7] There are rabbis who are attempting to reinstitute this ancient custom. Like all customs, it will have to pass the test of public acceptance.

BRITH MILAH CUSTOMS

The custom of lighting candles at a *Brith Milah* originated at a time when it was illegal to perform a *brith.* A lighted candle during the daylight hours would silently announce that a *Brith Milah* was to take place in this locale. Jews passing by would enter to hear the blessings.[8] This custom has continued on a limited basis whether the *Brith Milah* takes place in the synagogue or at home.[9]

There was a time when Jews spread a cloth on the door of the synagogue to signal the fact that a *Brith Milah* was to take place.[10]

The Sephardic community in Jerusalem has a custom of enjoying the scent of myrtle at a *Brith Milah.* The sexton brings a copper tray filled with branches of spices. A blessing is pronounced for the spices in addition to the customary blessing over the wine. This is very similar to the *Havdalah,* which marks the conclusion of the Sabbath, when blessings for the wine and spices are made. The origin of this custom is unknown. One authority suggests that it began in the days of the Spanish Inquisition. The sweet aroma of the spices encouraged passing Jews to have courage. Jewish parents were endangering their lives by obeying God's commandment to circumcise their child.[11]

THE BABY'S DRESS

It is customary to dress the baby in attire befitting the occasion of being blessed by the prophet Elijah, who is present at every *Brith Milah,* and entering the covenant with his Creator.[12] The Talmud comments: "'This is my God, and I will adorn Him.'[13] Make a beautiful *sukkah* in His honor, have a beautiful *lulav,* a beautiful *shofar,* beautiful *tzitzith,* and a beautiful scroll of the Law."[14] Rashi adds that it is a *mitzvah* to make *Brith Milah* a beautiful and meaningful rite.[15]

TALITH AND TEPHILLIN

When a *Brith Milah* takes place in a synagogue at the conclusion of the Sabbath or festival services, it is customary that the worshippers remain adorned with their prayer-shawls (*Talithoth*); after the weekday service, one should not remove the prayer-shawl (*Talith*) or phylacteries (*Tephillin*).[16] Should the *Brith Milah* be long after the service, it is suggested that the three main participants, the father, *mohel,* and *sandek* wear prayer-shawls. This is not mandatory, but it adds to the beauty and the sanctity of the occasion.

THE BRITH MILAH

The *Brith Milah* can be accomplished with very few people in attendance. The only people required are the *mohel* and the *san-*

dek.[17] This can be reduced further to only one person, the *mohel.* It should be obvious that no apartment is too small to accommodate the *Brith Milah.*

When it is possible to perform the rite elaborately, this should be done, because it does honor to our faith. The presence of a *minyan* is recommended, but less than ten males will suffice.[18] A *minyan* is preferable because Elijah the prophet attends every *brith,* and it is fitting that there be a quorum in honor of such an exalted guest.

Two chairs are arranged side by side—one for Elijah and one for the *sandek,* who holds the baby.[19] A couple designated as *kvaterin* and *kvater* carry the baby on a pillow to the room where the *brith* will take place. The term *kvater* dates back to the Middle Ages and comes from the German *Gottvater,* "Godfather," which became *G'vater* and finally the term we use, *kvater.*[20] When the baby arrives, the guests rise and say *Barukh Haba,* "Blessed be he who enters."[21]

The father of the child says, "I am ready to perform the precept of circumcising my son, as the Creator, blessed be He, has commanded us in the Torah: 'Every male among you, throughout your generations, shall be circumcised when he is eight days old.' "[22]

The *mohel* places the infant in the chair designated for Elijah the prophet and says: "This is the throne of Elijah, of blessed memory."[23] All in attendance should offer a silent prayer that Elijah bless the infant. The *mohel* takes the baby from Elijah's chair and places him on a pillow on the knees of the *sandek.*

Sandek comes from the Greek *synteknos,* or the "helper" of the child.[24] The *sandek* holds the baby on his lap while the *mohel* fulfills his holy task. Another acceptable procedure is to place the baby on a table and have the *sandek* hold him securely.[25]

The person selected to be the *sandek* should be chosen with great care. There are different traditions governing the selection of the *sandek.* Families are often happy to honor the grandfather or the great-grandfather. This is in accordance with the tradition brought by the family from their country of origin. Other families give this honor to their rabbi.[26] Families that are not bound to any one tradition are at liberty to make their own selection. One must be mindful that the *sandek* is compared to a person offering a sacrifice and that his lap is an altar unto the Lord.[27]

The father of the infant, the *mohel,* and the *sandek* should regard this sacred occasion as a holiday.[28] They are permitted to be dressed in their Sabbath attire even during periods when this is forbidden to other Jews.

Because the *mohel* is fulfilling a task that rightfully belongs to the father of the child, it is customary that the father stand close by during the *Brith Milah,* to make it known that the *mohel* is his emissary.[29] This, however, is not obligatory.

The *mohel* then proceeds with the *Brith Milah.* (The service of *Brith Milah* is found in Chapter 10). At the conclusion of the ritual, the *kvater* takes the infant and returns him to his crib.

THE SEUDATH MITZVAH

It is customary to have a meal after the *brith.*[30] The meal is a *Seudath Mitzvah,* a meal sanctified by a *mitzvah,* because it is associated with *Brith Milah.* Due to the fact that the circumcision is usually performed in the morning, the meal may be a simple breakfast. The meal, or *seudah,* may take place at any time during the day, depending on when the *Brith Milah* occurs. This special meal affords the attendees the opportunity to say Grace After the Meal and to offer prayers on behalf of the newborn infant, his parents, and all the participants in the *mitzvah.*

Maimonides suggested the correct way to observe this religious repast, as well as all others in the life-cycle of a Jew.[31] When an individual partakes of the meal he is obliged to provide for poor people. If he locks the door to his home and eats and drinks with his family and friends and bars the unfortunate, this is not considered to be the joy of the *mitzvah* but rather the joy of his own gratification.

The meal is delayed when the *brith* takes place on a fast-day. Then the custom is to have the *brith* before sundown, which is followed by the evening service and the meal.[32]

Should a *brith* occur on the eve of a Sabbath, it is permissible to have the *Seudath Mitzvah* immediately after the *brith*.[33] Whenever possible, the *brith* should take place early in the morning. There are scholars who maintain that when the *brith* is on the eve of the Sabbath, the meal should be enjoyed on the Sabbath.[34]

BLESSINGS ARE SAID WITH A GOBLET OF WINE

Acts of holiness are sanctified with a goblet of wine; for example, the Sabbath and festival *Kiddush,* the wedding ceremony, and the blessings that are chanted at the *Brith Milah.* When no wine is available, other liquids are permissible.[35] It is an accepted practice that the person who recited the blessings drinks from the wine after dabbing the infant's lips with cotton that was placed in the wine.

A FATHER WHO CANNOT READ THE BLESSINGS

One scholar stated that when the father cannot read Hebrew, the *sandek* should pronounce the blessings in his stead.[36] Another authority offers the generally accepted custom that someone pronounce the blessings and the father repeat the words after him.[37] A third opinion recommends that we follow the practice of the marriage ceremony, where the betrothal blessings are intoned by the officiating rabbi, when in actuality they should be said by the bridegroom. The reason that the rabbi says all the blessings is to avoid embarrassing a bridegroom who does not know how to read the blessings.[38]

In order to eliminate the possibility of embarrassment to the father, a transliteration of the blessings along with a translation and brief commentary will be offered in Chapter 10.

When the father is not present at the *Brith Milah,* the custom is for the *sandek* to say the blessings for the father.[39]

SHE'HE'CHE'YANU

She'he'che'yanu ("Who granted us life"), the blessing of

thanksgiving that God has permitted us to reach a very special occasion, is omitted at a *brith*. Sephardic Jews follow the decision rendered by Maimonides that this blessing should be said at a *brith*.[40] Rabbi Moshe Isserles states:

> In these lands it is customary to omit the prayer even when the father serves as the *mohel*, unless the child is a first-born who is to be redeemed. In such cases the father recites the blessing at the *brith* and omits it at the redemption-of-the-first-born ceremony. If the child does not have to be redeemed, the prayer is not said at the *brith*.[41]

The practice is not to say this prayer in any circumstance. The reason, according to the rabbis, is that there is a very slight possibility that the baby might have pain during the *Brith Milah*. Actually, this concern is not realistic. Since the infant's nervous system is still undeveloped, he does not feel any pain. The baby cries because he objects to any annoyance.

CIRCUMCISION OF TWINS

When twins are to be circumcised, each child is treated individually. The blessings are recited separately for each child.[42] It is, however, permissible to say the blessings once and to include both children.[43]

The latter procedure can be accomplished by having in mind both children when the blessings are said, and avoiding extraneous conversations between the circumcisions. In such an instance the blessings are recited in the plural form: "to introduce them" (*L'hakhnisam*) rather than "to introduce him." The *mohel's* blessings would also be in the plural: "sustain the children" (*kayaim eth hayeladim*) for their father and mother.

Since both procedures are correct, each community should follow its established custom, whether to circumcise with individual or joint rituals. A community that does not have an established custom would be advised to have each *Brith Milah* performed separately.

9

Texts on Brith Milah

God appeared to Abram when he was ninety-nine years old and said, "I am God Almighty; walk before Me and be a complete man. I will establish My *brith* between us, and I will multiply you." Abram fell on his face; and God continued to speak, "My *brith* is with you, and you shall become the father of a multitude of nations. Your name shall no longer be Abram, but your name shall be Abraham; for I will make you the father of a multitude of nations. You shall be very fruitful. Nations and kings shall come forth from you. My *brith* will be established with you and your descendants for an everlasting *brith*. I will be your God and the God of your descendants. I hereby give you and to your descendants all the land of Canaan, for an eternal possession. You and your descendants shall keep My *brith* forever. This is My covenant. Every male shall be circumcised. You shall circumcise the flesh of your foreskin, and it shall be a sign of the *brith* between us. Every male shall be circumcised when he is eight days old."[1]

The uncircumcised male shall be cut off from his people; he has broken My covenant.[2]

God said [to Abraham], "Your wife Sarah shall bear you a son, and you shall name him Isaac. I will establish My *brith* with him as an everlasting covenant and with his descendants after him."[3]

Abraham circumcised his son Isaac when he was eight days old, as God commanded him to do.[4]

Zipporah circumcised her son and cast the foreskin towards the feet of Moses, and said, "Surely you are a bridegroom of blood to me."[5]

The uncircumcised may not eat of the Passover sacrifice.[6]

The foreskin shall be circumcised on the eighth day.[7]

I will be gracious to you [the Jewish people]. I will make you fruitful and successful, and I will always keep My covenant with you.[8]

The Lord said to Joshua, "Prepare instruments and circumcise the Children of Israel." So Joshua made the instruments and circumcised the Children of Israel at Gibeath-haaraloth. And this is the reason why Joshua circumcised them. All the males who left Egypt died in the wilderness. Though all the Jewish males who left Egypt had been circumcised, yet those who were born in the wilderness had not been circumcised. Those who left Egypt were not permitted to see the land that was promised to their forefathers, the land flowing with milk and honey, because they had disobeyed the Lord. Joshua circumcised the males who were born in the wilderness because they were not circumcised on the journey.[9]

[The prophet Elijah said], "I have been zealous for the Lord, the God of hosts, because the Children of Israel have forsaken the *brith,* they have destroyed the altars and slain Your prophets with the sword. I am the sole remnant and they want to take my life."[10]

Do not spurn us, for Your name's sake; do not dishonor Your glorious throne; remember and do not break Your *brith* with us.[11]

I will make an eternal *brith* with My people and they will always remain faithful to Me.[12]

Thus said the Lord, "Were it not for the *brith,* the laws governing day and night, heaven and earth would not have been established."[13]

The princes as well as the entire household of Israel accepted the *brith* as a mandate to set their slaves free, never to be enslaved again.[14]

They shall ask the route to Zion, saying, "Let us visit the Lord with whom we have an eternal *brith.*"[15]

10

The Service at a Circumcision
סֵדֶר בְּרִית מִילָה

When the child is brought in for the circumcision, those present at the ceremony rise and say:

בָּרוּךְ הַבָּא:

Barukh Haba.   Blessed is he who enters.[1]

The father of the child says:

הִנְנִי מוּכָן וּמְזֻמָּן לְקַיֵּם מִצְוַת עֲשֵׂה שֶׁצִּוָּנוּ הַבּוֹרֵא יִתְבָּרַךְ לָמוּל אֶת בְּנִי
כַּכָּתוּב בַּתּוֹרָה: וּבֶן־שְׁמוֹנַת יָמִים יִמּוֹל לָכֶם כָּל־זָכָר לְדֹרֹתֵיכֶם:

Hineni mukhan um'zuman l'kayaim mitzvath asai shetzivanu Haboreh yithbarakh lamul eth b'ni. Kakatuv ba'-Torah: "u'ven sh'monath yamim yimol la'khem kol zakhar l'do'rothaikhem."

I am ready to fulfill the *mitzvah* of circumcising my son, as the Creator, blessed be He, commanded us in the Torah: "Every male shall be circumcised when he is eight days old."[2]

The mohel takes the child and places him on a seat, and says:

זֶה הַכִּסֵּא שֶׁל אֵלִיָּהוּ זָכוּר לַטּוֹב: לִישׁוּעָתְךָ קִוִּיתִי יְיָ: שִׁבַּרְתִּי לִישׁוּעָתְךָ
יְיָ, וּמִצְוֹתֶיךָ עָשִׂיתִי: שִׁבַּרְתִּי לִישׁוּעָתְךָ יְיָ: שָׂשׂ אָנֹכִי עַל אִמְרָתֶךָ, כְּמוֹצֵא

51

שָׁלָל רָב. שָׁלוֹם רָב לְאֹהֲבֵי תוֹרָתֶךָ, וְאֵין לָמוֹ מִכְשׁוֹל: אַשְׁרֵי תִּבְחַר
וּתְקָרֵב יִשְׁכֹּן חֲצֵרֶיךָ.

Zeh hakisai shel Eliyahu—zakhur latov. "Lishu'athkha kivithi Adonoy. Sibarti lishu'athkha Adonoy, u'mitzvothekha asithi. Sibarti lishu'athkha Adonoy. Sas anokhi al imrathekha k'motzai sha'lal rav. Shalom rav l'ohavai Thorathekha v'ain lamo mikhshol. Ashrai tivchar u'thkaraiv chatzairekha."

This is the throne of Elijah—may he be remembered for good.[3] "I wait for Your salvation, O Lord. I wait for Your deliverance, and I have fulfilled Your commandments. I find joy in Your promise, like one who finds wealth. Those who love Your Torah enjoy peace and they do not stumble. Happy is the person whom You select to live in Your courts."[4]

Those present respond:

נִשְׂבְּעָה בְּטוּב בֵּיתֶךָ, קְדוֹשׁ הֵיכָלֶךָ:

"Nis'b'ah b'tuv baithekha, k'dosh hai'kha'le'kha."

"May we be satisfied with the goodness of Your house, Your Holy Temple."

The mohel takes the child from Elijah's throne, places the infant on the pillow on the knees of the sandek, and offers this blessing:

בָּרוּךְ אַתָּה יְיָ אֱלֹהֵינוּ מֶלֶךְ הָעוֹלָם. אֲשֶׁר קִדְּשָׁנוּ בְּמִצְוֹתָיו וְצִוָּנוּ עַל
הַמִּילָה:

Barukh ata Adonoy Elohainu Melekh ha'olam, asher kidshanu b'mitzvothav v'tzivanu al ha'milah.

Blessed are You, Lord our God, King of the universe, who sanctified us by Your commandments, and commanded us concerning circumcision.[5]

Immediately after the circumcision the father recites this blessing:

בָּרוּךְ אַתָּה יְיָ אֱלֹהֵינוּ מֶלֶךְ הָעוֹלָם. אֲשֶׁר קִדְּשָׁנוּ בְּמִצְוֹתָיו וְצִוָּנוּ לְהַכְנִיסוֹ בִּבְרִיתוֹ שֶׁל אַבְרָהָם אָבִינוּ:

Barukh ata Adonoy Elohainu Melekh ha'olam, asher kidshanu b'mitzvothav v'tzivanu l'hakhniso bivritho shel Avraham avinu.

Blessed are You, Lord our God, King of the universe, who sanctified us by Your commandments and commanded us to have our sons enter into the covenant of Abraham our father.[6]

Those present respond:

כְּשֵׁם שֶׁנִּכְנַס לַבְּרִית, כֵּן יִכָּנֵס לְתוֹרָה וּלְחֻפָּה וּלְמַעֲשִׂים טוֹבִים:

K'shaim she'nikhnas la'brith kain yikanais l'Torah u'l'chupah u'l'ma'asim tovim.

Even as this child has entered into the covenant, so may he enter into the study of the Torah, the wedding canopy, and to good deeds.[7]

The child is handed to one of those present, and the mohel, taking up a cup of wine, continues:

בָּרוּךְ אַתָּה יְיָ אֱלֹהֵינוּ מֶלֶךְ הָעוֹלָם, בּוֹרֵא פְּרִי הַגָּפֶן:

Barukh ata Adonoy Elohainu Melekh ha'olam, borai pri hagafen.

Blessed are You, Lord our God, King of the universe, who creates the fruit of the vine.[8]

בָּרוּךְ אַתָּה יְיָ אֱלֹהֵינוּ מֶלֶךְ הָעוֹלָם. אֲשֶׁר קִדֵּשׁ יָדִיד מִבֶּטֶן וְחֹק בִּשְׁאֵרוֹ שָׂם. וְצֶאֱצָאָיו חָתַם בְּאוֹת בְּרִית קֹדֶשׁ. עַל כֵּן בִּשְׂכַר זֹאת. אֵל חַי חֶלְקֵנוּ צוּרֵנוּ. צַוֵּה לְהַצִּיל יְדִידוּת שְׁאֵרֵנוּ מִשַּׁחַת. לְמַעַן בְּרִיתוֹ אֲשֶׁר שָׂם בִּבְשָׂרֵנוּ. בָּרוּךְ אַתָּה יְיָ. כּוֹרֵת הַבְּרִית:

Barukh ata Adonoy Elohainu Melekh ha'olam asher kidaish y'did mibeten v'chok bishairo sam v'tze'etza'av chatham b'oth brith kodesh, al kain biskhar zoth, El chay chelkainu tzurainu, tzavai l'hatzil y'diduth sh'airainu mishachath, l'ma'an b'ritho asher sam biv'sa'rainu. Barukh ata Adonoy koraith habrith.

Blessed are You, Lord our God, King of the universe, who did sanctify the beloved person[9] from birth, impressing Your statute in his flesh and marking his descendants with the sign of the holy covenant. Because of this, for the sake of the covenant, Eternal God, our Stronghold, deliver our dearly beloved from destruction. Blessed are You, O Lord, partner to the covenant.

אֱלֹהֵינוּ וֵאלֹהֵי אֲבוֹתֵינוּ. קַיֵּם אֶת הַיֶּלֶד הַזֶּה לְאָבִיו וּלְאִמּוֹ. וְיִקָּרֵא שְׁמוֹ בְּיִשְׂרָאֵל (פְּלוֹנִי בֶּן פְּלוֹנִי). יִשְׂמַח הָאָב בְּיוֹצֵא חֲלָצָיו. וְתָגֵל אִמּוֹ בִּפְרִי בִטְנָהּ. כַּכָּתוּב: יִשְׂמַח אָבִיךָ וְאִמֶּךָ וְתָגֵל יוֹלַדְתֶּךָ. וְנֶאֱמַר: וָאֶעֱבוֹר עָלַיִךְ וָאֶרְאֵךְ מִתְבּוֹסֶסֶת בְּדָמָיִךְ, וָאֹמַר לָךְ בְּדָמַיִךְ חֲיִי, וָאֹמַר לָךְ בְּדָמַיִךְ חֲיִי. וְנֶאֱמַר: זָכַר לְעוֹלָם בְּרִיתוֹ, דָּבָר צִוָּה לְאֶלֶף דּוֹר. אֲשֶׁר כָּרַת אֶת אַבְרָהָם וּשְׁבוּעָתוֹ לְיִצְחָק. וַיַּעֲמִידֶהָ לְיַעֲקֹב לְחֹק לְיִשְׂרָאֵל בְּרִית עוֹלָם. וְנֶאֱמַר: וַיָּמָל אַבְרָהָם אֶת יִצְחָק בְּנוֹ בֶּן שְׁמֹנַת יָמִים כַּאֲשֶׁר צִוָּה אֹתוֹ אֱלֹהִים. הוֹדוּ לַיְיָ כִּי טוֹב כִּי לְעוֹלָם חַסְדּוֹ. זֶה הַקָּטֹן (פְּלוֹנִי) גָּדוֹל יִהְיֶה. כְּשֵׁם שֶׁנִּכְנַס לַבְּרִית, כֵּן יִכָּנֵס לְתוֹרָה וּלְחֻפָּה וּלְמַעֲשִׂים טוֹבִים:

Elohainu Vai'lohai Avothainu, kayaim eth ha'yeled hazeh l'aviv ul'imo, v'yikarai sh'mo b'Yisrael . . . ben . . . . Yismach ha'av b'yotzai chalatzav, v'thagail imo b'fri vitna, kakathuv: "Yismach, a'vikha v'imekha v'thagail yo'ladthekha." V'ne'emar: "Va'e'evor a'la'yikh va'er'aikh mith'boseses b'damayikh,

Our God and God of our fathers, preserve this child to his father and to his mother,[10] and let his name[11] be called in Israel . . . the son of . . . . May father and mother rejoice in their offspring, as it is written: "Let your parents be happy; let your mother thrill with joy." "I passed by you and saw you

va'omar lakh b'damayikh cha'yi; va'omar lakh b'damayikh cha'yi." V'ne'emar: "Zakhar l'olam britho, davar tzivah l'elef dor. Asher karath eth Avraham, ush'vu'atho l'Yitzchak. Va'ya'a'mideha l'Yaakov l'chok, l'Yisrael brith olam." V'ne'emar: "Va'yamal Avraham eth Yitzchak b'no ben sh'monath yamim, ka'asher tzivah otho Elohim." "Hodu La'Adonoy ki tov, ki l'olam chasdo." Zeh hakatan . . . gadol y'h'yeh. K'shaim she'nikhnas la'brith, kain y'kanais l'Torah, l'chupah u'l'ma'asim tovim.

soaking in your blood. I said to you 'live through your blood.' "[12] "He remembers His covenant forever, the word which He pledged for a thousand generations, the covenant He made with Abraham, and His oath to Isaac. He confirmed it to Jacob as a statute, to Israel as an everlasting covenant." It is written: "Abraham circumcised his son Isaac when he was eight days old, as God commanded him." "Give thanks to the Lord, for He is good; His mercy endures forever." May this child, named . . ., mature properly. Even as he has entered into the covenant, so may he enter into the study of the Torah, the wedding canopy, and to a life of good deeds.

The mohel drinks of the wine; a few drops are given to the infant, and the Cup of Blessing is offered to the mother.

11

Grace after Brith Milah and Pidyon Haben
בִּרְכַּת הַמָּזוֹן

Upon washing the hands before meals:

Blessed are You, Lord our God, King of the universe, who sanctified us with Your commandments, and commanded us concerning the washing of the hands.[1]

בָּרוּךְ אַתָּה יְיָ אֱלֹהֵינוּ מֶלֶךְ הָעוֹלָם, אֲשֶׁר קִדְּשָׁנוּ בְּמִצְוֹתָיו וְצִוָּנוּ עַל נְטִילַת יָדָיִם.

Over bread:

Blessed are You, Lord our God, King of the universe, who brings forth bread from the earth.[2]

בָּרוּךְ אַתָּה יְיָ אֱלֹהֵינוּ מֶלֶךְ הָעוֹלָם הַמּוֹצִיא לֶחֶם מִן הָאָרֶץ.

During the *Seudath Mitzvah* (meal) after the *Brith Milah*, it is the practice in many congregations to chant a *piyut* (liturgical poem).[3] When the meal is concluded, the assembled guests say Grace,[4] which is introduced with Psalm 126.[5]

A Song of Ascent

When the Lord brought the exiles back to Zion, we were like in a dream. Our mouths were filled with laughter, and a song of exultation was on our tongues. Then they said among the nations, "The Lord has done great things for them." The Lord has done great things for us, and we rejoiced. Restore our fortunes, Lord, like streams in the Negev. They who sow in tears will reap in joy. He who goes forth weeping, carrying the seed for sowing, shall come home with joy, carrying his sheaves.

שִׁיר הַמַּעֲלוֹת. בְּשׁוּב יְיָ אֶת־שִׁיבַת צִיּוֹן הָיִינוּ כְּחֹלְמִים. אָז יִמָּלֵא שְׂחוֹק פִּינוּ, וּלְשׁוֹנֵנוּ רִנָּה; אָז יֹאמְרוּ בַגּוֹיִם, הִגְדִּיל יְיָ לַעֲשׂוֹת עִם־אֵלֶּה. הִגְדִּיל יְיָ לַעֲשׂוֹת עִמָּנוּ, הָיִינוּ שְׂמֵחִים. שׁוּבָה יְיָ אֶת־שְׁבִיתֵנוּ, כַּאֲפִיקִים בַּנֶּגֶב. הַזֹּרְעִים בְּדִמְעָה, בְּרִנָּה יִקְצֹרוּ. הָלוֹךְ יֵלֵךְ וּבָכֹה, נֹשֵׂא מֶשֶׁךְ־הַזָּרַע; בֹּא־יָבֹא בְרִנָּה נֹשֵׂא אֲלֻמֹּתָיו.

It is customary for those assembled to pour water on their fingertips in preparation for Grace.[6] A cup is filled with wine and placed in the hand of the one selected to lead in saying Grace.[7]

The following invitation to say Grace is said at the meal celebrating a *Brith Milah*. The next invitation to say Grace is said at all occasions except at a wedding.

Leader:

Friends, Let us say Grace.[8]

רַבּוֹתַי, נְבָרֵךְ.

Company and then Leader:

May the name of the Lord be praised now and forever.[9]

יְהִי שֵׁם יְיָ מְבֹרָךְ מֵעַתָּה וְעַד עוֹלָם.

All:

Praise God, provider of all blessing.

נוֹדֶה לְשִׁמְךָ בְּתוֹךְ אֱמוּנָי, בְּרוּכִים אַתֶּם לַיְיָ.

Leader:

We ask permission of God, who reigns from on high.

בִּרְשׁוּת אֵל אָיוֹם וְנוֹרָא, מִשְׂגָּב לְעִתּוֹת בַּצָּרָה, אֵל נֶאְזָר בִּגְבוּרָה, אַדִּיר בַּמָּרוֹם יְיָ.

All:

Praise God, provider of all blessing.

נוֹדֶה לְשִׁמְךָ בְּתוֹךְ אֱמוּנָי, בְּרוּכִים אַתֶּם לַיְיָ.

Leader:

We ask permission of the sacred Torah, which we received from Moses, Servant of God.

בִּרְשׁוּת הַתּוֹרָה הַקְּדוֹשָׁה, טְהוֹרָה הִיא וְגַם פְּרוּשָׁה, צִוָּה לָנוּ מוֹרָשָׁה, מֹשֶׁה עֶבֶד יְיָ.

All:

Praise God, provider of all blessing.

נוֹדֶה לְשִׁמְךָ בְּתוֹךְ אֱמוּנָי, בְּרוּכִים אַתֶּם לַיְיָ.

Leader:

We ask permission of the *Cohanim* and Levites to exalt God.

בִּרְשׁוּת הַכֹּהֲנִים הַלְוִיִּם, אֶקְרָא לֵאלֹהֵי הָעִבְרִיִּים, אֲהוֹדֶנּוּ בְּכָל אִיִּים, אֲבָרְכָה אֶת יְיָ.

All:

Praise God, provider of all blessing.

נוֹדֶה לְשִׁמְךָ בְּתוֹךְ אֱמוּנָי, בְּרוּכִים אַתֶּם לַיְיָ.

Leader:

We ask permission to exclaim: blessed is he who comes in the name of the Lord.

בִּרְשׁוּת מוֹרַי וְרַבּוֹתַי, אֶפְתַּח בְּשִׁיר פִּי וּשְׂפָתַי, וְתֹאמַרְנָה עַצְמוֹתַי, בָּרוּךְ הַבָּא בְּשֵׁם יְיָ.

All:

Praise God, provider of all blessing.

נוֹדֶה לְשִׁמְךָ בְּתוֹךְ אֱמוּנָי, בְּרוּכִים אַתֶּם לַיְיָ.

The words in parentheses are included when a *minyan* is present. This invitation is said at a *Pidyon Haben*. At a *Brith Milah* omit the following two sentences:

Leader·

Friends, let us say Grace.[8]

רַבּוֹתַי, נְבָרֵךְ.

Company, then leader:

May the name of the Lord be praised now and forever.[9]

יְהִי שֵׁם יְיָ מְבֹרָךְ מֵעַתָּה וְעַד עוֹלָם.

Leader:

With your consent, let us bless (our) God whose food we have eaten.[10]

בִּרְשׁוּת מָרָנָן וְרַבָּנָן וְרַבּוֹתַי נְבָרֵךְ (אֱלֹהֵינוּ) שֶׁאָכַלְנוּ מִשֶּׁלּוֹ.

Company, then leader:

Praised be (our) God of whose bounty we have partaken and by whose goodness we are sustained.[11]

בָּרוּךְ (אֱלֹהֵינוּ) שֶׁאָכַלְנוּ מִשֶּׁלּוֹ וּבְטוּבוֹ חָיִינוּ.

All:

Blessed be He and Blessed be His name.

בָּרוּךְ הוּא וּבָרוּךְ שְׁמוֹ:

We praise and bless You, Lord our God, King of the universe. In Your goodness You sustain the entire world with graciousness, kindness, and compassion. You provide food for all humanity. Your mercy is infinite. Because of Your goodness, we have never been in want of food. O may we never be in want of it, for Your name's sake. You sustain everyone, You do good to all, and You provide food for all whom You have created. Blessed are You, Lord, who provides for everyone.[12]

בָּרוּךְ אַתָּה יְיָ אֱלֹהֵינוּ מֶלֶךְ הָעוֹלָם, הַזָּן אֶת הָעוֹלָם כֻּלּוֹ בְּטוּבוֹ, בְּחֵן בְּחֶסֶד וּבְרַחֲמִים. הוּא נוֹתֵן לֶחֶם לְכָל בָּשָׂר, כִּי לְעוֹלָם חַסְדּוֹ. וּבְטוּבוֹ הַגָּדוֹל תָּמִיד לֹא חָסַר לָנוּ, וְאַל יֶחְסַר לָנוּ מָזוֹן לְעוֹלָם וָעֶד בַּעֲבוּר שְׁמוֹ הַגָּדוֹל. כִּי הוּא אֵל זָן וּמְפַרְנֵס לַכֹּל, וּמֵטִיב לַכֹּל, וּמֵכִין מָזוֹן לְכָל בְּרִיּוֹתָיו אֲשֶׁר בָּרָא. בָּרוּךְ אַתָּה, יְיָ, הַזָּן אֶת הַכֹּל.

We thank You, Lord our God, for having given our fathers a good and ample land, and for having liberated us from Egyptian bondage. We thank You for the *Brith Milah* which is sealed in our flesh, for the Torah You

נוֹדֶה לְּךָ, יְיָ אֱלֹהֵינוּ, עַל שֶׁהִנְחַלְתָּ לַאֲבוֹתֵינוּ אֶרֶץ חֶמְדָּה טוֹבָה וּרְחָבָה; וְעַל שֶׁהוֹצֵאתָנוּ יְיָ אֱלֹהֵינוּ, מֵאֶרֶץ מִצְרַיִם, וּפְדִיתָנוּ מִבֵּית עֲבָדִים; וְעַל בְּרִיתְךָ שֶׁחָתַמְתָּ בִּבְשָׂרֵנוּ; וְעַל תּוֹרָתְךָ שֶׁלִּמַּדְתָּנוּ;

imparted to us, for the laws which You gave us, and for the gift of life which has been mercifully bestowed on us. We are thankful for the food You provide us at all times.[13]

וְעַל חֻקֶּיךָ שֶׁהוֹדַעְתָּנוּ; וְעַל חַיִּים, חֵן וָחֶסֶד שֶׁחוֹנַנְתָּנוּ; וְעַל אֲכִילַת מָזוֹן שָׁאַתָּה זָן וּמְפַרְנֵס אוֹתָנוּ תָּמִיד, בְּכָל יוֹם וּבְכָל עֵת וּבְכָל שָׁעָה.

On Chanukah and Purim:

We thank You for the miraculous victories which You performed for our ancestors at this season of the year.

עַל הַנִּסִּים וְעַל הַפֻּרְקָן, וְעַל הַגְּבוּרוֹת וְעַל הַתְּשׁוּעוֹת, וְעַל הַמִּלְחָמוֹת, שֶׁעָשִׂיתָ לַאֲבוֹתֵינוּ בַּיָּמִים הָהֵם בַּזְּמַן הַזֶּה.

On Chanukah:

In the days of the Hasmonean, Mattathias ben Yochanan, the High Priest, and his sons, the wicked Hellenic empire attempted to force Israel to forsake the Torah and to transgress Your laws. You protected Israel during this ordeal. You delivered the mighty into the hands of the weak; the numerous into the hands of the few; the corrupt into the hands of the pure; the wicked into the hands of the righteous; and the arrogant into the hands of the faithful.

You gained recognition with this great deliverance.

Thereupon Your children re-

בִּימֵי מַתִּתְיָהוּ בֶּן יוֹחָנָן כֹּהֵן גָּדוֹל, חַשְׁמוֹנִי וּבָנָיו, כְּשֶׁעָמְדָה מַלְכוּת יָוָן הָרְשָׁעָה עַל עַמְּךָ יִשְׂרָאֵל לְהַשְׁכִּיחָם תּוֹרָתֶךָ, וּלְהַעֲבִירָם מֵחֻקֵּי רְצוֹנֶךָ. וְאַתָּה בְּרַחֲמֶיךָ הָרַבִּים עָמַדְתָּ לָהֶם בְּעֵת צָרָתָם, רַבְתָּ אֶת רִיבָם, דַּנְתָּ אֶת דִּינָם, נָקַמְתָּ אֶת נִקְמָתָם, מָסַרְתָּ גִבּוֹרִים בְּיַד חַלָּשִׁים, וְרַבִּים בְּיַד מְעַטִּים, וּטְמֵאִים בְּיַד טְהוֹרִים, וּרְשָׁעִים בְּיַד צַדִּיקִים, וְזֵדִים בְּיַד עוֹסְקֵי תוֹרָתֶךָ. וּלְךָ עָשִׂיתָ שֵׁם גָּדוֹל וְקָדוֹשׁ בְּעוֹלָמֶךָ, וּלְעַמְּךָ יִשְׂרָאֵל עָשִׂיתָ תְּשׁוּעָה גְדוֹלָה וּפֻרְקָן כְּהַיּוֹם הַזֶּה. וְאַחַר כֵּן בָּאוּ בָנֶיךָ לִדְבִיר בֵּיתֶךָ,

dedicated the Temple, kindled lights in the holy courts, and designated these eight days of Chanukah for giving thanks and praise to Your great name.[14]

וּפִנּוּ אֶת הֵיכָלֶךָ, וְטִהֲרוּ אֶת מִקְדָּשֶׁךָ, וְהִדְלִיקוּ נֵרוֹת בְּחַצְרוֹת קָדְשֶׁךָ, וְקָבְעוּ שְׁמוֹנַת יְמֵי חֲנֻכָּה אֵלּוּ לְהוֹדוֹת וּלְהַלֵּל לְשִׁמְךָ הַגָּדוֹל.

On Purim:

During the time of Mordecai and Esther, in Shushan, the capital of Persia, Haman rose up against Your people. He wanted to annihilate them on the thirteenth day of Adar, and to plunder their wealth. You mercifully frustrated his plans. Haman and his sons were punished for their cruel deeds.[15]

בִּימֵי מָרְדְּכַי וְאֶסְתֵּר בְּשׁוּשַׁן הַבִּירָה, כְּשֶׁעָמַד עֲלֵיהֶם הָמָן הָרָשָׁע. בִּקֵּשׁ לְהַשְׁמִיד לַהֲרֹג וּלְאַבֵּד אֶת כָּל הַיְּהוּדִים, מִנַּעַר וְעַד זָקֵן, טַף וְנָשִׁים בְּיוֹם אֶחָד, בִּשְׁלוֹשָׁה עָשָׂר לְחֹדֶשׁ שְׁנֵים עָשָׂר, הוּא חֹדֶשׁ אֲדָר, וּשְׁלָלָם לָבוֹז. וְאַתָּה בְּרַחֲמֶיךָ הָרַבִּים הֵפַרְתָּ אֶת עֲצָתוֹ, וְקִלְקַלְתָּ אֶת מַחֲשַׁבְתּוֹ, וַהֲשֵׁבוֹתָ גְּמוּלוֹ בְּרֹאשׁוֹ, וְתָלוּ אוֹתוֹ וְאֶת בָּנָיו עַל הָעֵץ.

We acclaim You, Lord our God, for all Your kindness. May every living being praise Your name forever. As it is written: "When you have eaten and are satisfied, you shall praise the Lord your God for the good land He has given you." Bless the Lord, for the land and for its produce.[16]

וְעַל הַכֹּל, יְיָ אֱלֹהֵינוּ, אֲנַחְנוּ מוֹדִים לָךְ וּמְבָרְכִים אוֹתָךְ, יִתְבָּרַךְ שִׁמְךָ בְּפִי כָּל חַי תָּמִיד לְעוֹלָם וָעֶד, כַּכָּתוּב: וְאָכַלְתָּ וְשָׂבָעְתָּ, וּבֵרַכְתָּ אֶת יְיָ אֱלֹהֶיךָ עַל הָאָרֶץ הַטּוֹבָה אֲשֶׁר נָתַן לָךְ. בָּרוּךְ אַתָּה, יְיָ, עַל הָאָרֶץ וְעַל הַמָּזוֹן.

Have mercy, Lord our God, on Israel, on Jerusalem, on

רַחֵם, יְיָ אֱלֹהֵינוּ, עַל יִשְׂרָאֵל עַמֶּךָ, וְעַל יְרוּשָׁלַיִם עִירֶךָ, וְעַל צִיּוֹן

Zion, on the royal house of
David, and on the Holy Temple.

God, our Father, feed us, sustain and support us, and deliver
us from afflictions. May we
never be dependent on the gifts
of men, nor their favors, but
rather on Your generous hand.
Save us from shame and embarrassment.[17]

מִשְׁכַּן כְּבוֹדֶךָ, וְעַל מַלְכוּת בֵּית דָּוִד
מְשִׁיחֶךָ, וְעַל הַבַּיִת הַגָּדוֹל וְהַקָּדוֹשׁ
שֶׁנִּקְרָא שִׁמְךָ עָלָיו. אֱלֹהֵינוּ אָבִינוּ,
רְעֵנוּ זוּנֵנוּ, פַּרְנְסֵנוּ וְכַלְכְּלֵנוּ
וְהַרְוִיחֵנוּ, וְהַרְוַח לָנוּ, יְיָ אֱלֹהֵינוּ,
מְהֵרָה מִכָּל צָרוֹתֵינוּ. וְנָא אַל
תַּצְרִיכֵנוּ, יְיָ אֱלֹהֵינוּ, לֹא לִידֵי
מַתְּנַת בָּשָׂר וָדָם וְלֹא לִידֵי
הַלְוָאָתָם, כִּי אִם לְיָדְךָ הַמְּלֵאָה
הַפְּתוּחָה, הַקְּדוֹשָׁה וְהָרְחָבָה, שֶׁלֹּא
נֵבוֹשׁ וְלֹא נִכָּלֵם לְעוֹלָם וָעֶד.

On Sabbath:

Lord our God, strengthen us
by Your commandments, above
all by the commandment of the
holy Sabbath. On this day we
are to refrain from work and to
enjoy the delight of repose.
Spare us from grief on the day
of rest. May we be privileged to
see Zion comforted and the holy
city rebuilt. You are the source
of salvation and consolation.[18]

רְצֵה וְהַחֲלִיצֵנוּ, יְיָ אֱלֹהֵינוּ,
בְּמִצְוֹתֶיךָ וּבְמִצְוַת יוֹם הַשְּׁבִיעִי,
הַשַּׁבָּת הַגָּדוֹל וְהַקָּדוֹשׁ הַזֶּה; כִּי יוֹם
זֶה גָּדוֹל וְקָדוֹשׁ הוּא לְפָנֶיךָ, לִשְׁבָּת
בּוֹ וְלָנוּחַ בּוֹ בְּאַהֲבָה כְּמִצְוַת
רְצוֹנֶךָ. וּבִרְצוֹנְךָ הָנַח לָנוּ, יְיָ
אֱלֹהֵינוּ, שֶׁלֹּא תְהֵא צָרָה, וְיָגוֹן
וַאֲנָחָה, בְּיוֹם מְנוּחָתֵנוּ. וְהַרְאֵנוּ, יְיָ
אֱלֹהֵינוּ, בְּנֶחָמַת צִיּוֹן עִירֶךָ, וּבְבִנְיַן
יְרוּשָׁלַיִם עִיר קָדְשֶׁךָ, כִּי אַתָּה הוּא
בַּעַל הַיְשׁוּעוֹת וּבַעַל הַנֶּחָמוֹת.

On Rosh Chodesh and Festivals:

Our God and God of our
fathers, may the remembrance

אֱלֹהֵינוּ וֵאלֹהֵי אֲבוֹתֵינוּ, יַעֲלֶה
וְיָבֹא, וְיַגִּיעַ וְיֵרָאֶה, וְיֵרָצֶה וְיִשָּׁמַע,

of us and our fathers, of the Messiah and Jerusalem be accepted by You for deliverance and grace, kindness and mercy, for life and peace, on this day of

וְיִפָּקֵד וְיִזָּכֵר זִכְרוֹנֵנוּ וּפִקְדוֹנֵנוּ, וְזִכְרוֹן אֲבוֹתֵינוּ, וְזִכְרוֹן מָשִׁיחַ בֶּן דָּוִד עַבְדֶּךָ, וְזִכְרוֹן יְרוּשָׁלַיִם עִיר קָדְשֶׁךָ, וְזִכְרוֹן כָּל עַמְּךָ בֵּית יִשְׂרָאֵל לְפָנֶיךָ. לִפְלֵיטָה וּלְטוֹבָה, לְחֵן וּלְחֶסֶד וּלְרַחֲמִים, לְחַיִּים וּלְשָׁלוֹם, בְּיוֹם

Rosh Chodesh:

Rosh Chodesh ראשׁ הַחֹדֶשׁ

Pesach

the Feast of Matzoth חַג הַמַּצּוֹת

Shavuoth

Shavuoth חַג הַשָּׁבֻעוֹת

Rosh Hashanah

Remembrance הַזִּכָּרוֹן

Sukkoth

Tabernacles חַג הַסֻּכּוֹת

Shemini Atzereth

Eighth-Day Feast הַשְּׁמִינִי, חַג הָעֲצֶרֶת

Remember us this day, Lord our God, for life and well-being. We put our trust in You, our King, for You are gracious and merciful.[19]

הַזֶּה. זָכְרֵנוּ, יְיָ אֱלֹהֵינוּ, בּוֹ לְטוֹבָה, וּפָקְדֵנוּ בּוֹ לִבְרָכָה, וְהוֹשִׁיעֵנוּ בּוֹ לְחַיִּים. וּבִדְבַר יְשׁוּעָה וְרַחֲמִים חוּס וְחָנֵּנוּ, וְרַחֵם עָלֵינוּ וְהוֹשִׁיעֵנוּ כִּי אֵלֶיךָ עֵינֵינוּ, כִּי אֵל מֶלֶךְ חַנּוּן וְרַחוּם אָתָּה.

Rebuild Jerusalem, the holy וּבְנֵה יְרוּשָׁלַיִם עִיר הַקֹּדֶשׁ בִּמְהֵרָה

city, speedily in our time.
Blessed are You, the merciful
restorer of Jerusalem. Amen.[20]

בְּיָמֵינוּ. בָּרוּךְ אַתָּה, יְיָ, בּוֹנֵה בְרַחֲמָיו יְרוּשָׁלָיִם, אָמֵן.

Blessed are You, Lord our
God, King of the universe. You
are our God, our Father, our
Creator, our Redeemer, our
Shepherd. You are the good
King who showers kindness on
all. You constantly bestow on us
grace and kindness, compassion
and deliverance, life and peace.
May You never withhold Your
blessings from us.[21]

בָּרוּךְ אַתָּה, יְיָ אֱלֹהֵינוּ, מֶלֶךְ הָעוֹלָם, הָאֵל, אָבִינוּ, מַלְכֵּנוּ, אַדִּירֵנוּ, בּוֹרְאֵנוּ, גּוֹאֲלֵנוּ, יוֹצְרֵנוּ, קְדוֹשֵׁנוּ קְדוֹשׁ יַעֲקֹב, רוֹעֵנוּ, רוֹעֵה יִשְׂרָאֵל, הַמֶּלֶךְ הַטּוֹב וְהַמֵּטִיב לַכֹּל, שֶׁבְּכָל יוֹם וָיוֹם הוּא הֵטִיב, הוּא מֵטִיב, הוּא יֵיטִיב לָנוּ. הוּא גְמָלָנוּ, הוּא גוֹמְלֵנוּ, הוּא יִגְמְלֵנוּ לָעַד, לְחֵן וּלְחֶסֶד וּלְרַחֲמִים וּלְרֶוַח, הַצָּלָה וְהַצְלָחָה, בְּרָכָה וִישׁוּעָה, נֶחָמָה, פַּרְנָסָה וְכַלְכָּלָה, וְרַחֲמִים וְחַיִּים וְשָׁלוֹם וְכָל טוֹב, וּמִכָּל טוֹב לְעוֹלָם אַל יְחַסְּרֵנוּ.

May the Merciful One rule
over us forever.

הָרַחֲמָן, הוּא יִמְלוֹךְ עָלֵינוּ לְעוֹלָם וָעֶד.

May the Merciful One be
blessed in heaven and on earth.

הָרַחֲמָן, הוּא יִתְבָּרַךְ בַּשָּׁמַיִם וּבָאָרֶץ.

May the Merciful One be
praised throughout all generations, and may He be glorified
through us forever.

הָרַחֲמָן, הוּא יִשְׁתַּבַּח לְדוֹר דּוֹרִים, וְיִתְפָּאַר בָּנוּ לָעַד וּלְנֵצַח נְצָחִים, וְיִתְהַדַּר בָּנוּ לָעַד וּלְעוֹלְמֵי עוֹלָמִים.

May the Merciful One help
us support ourselves respect-
ably.

הָרַחֲמָן, הוּא יְפַרְנְסֵנוּ בְּכָבוֹד.

May the Merciful One remove the yoke from our neck; and lead us proudly to our country.

הָרַחֲמָן, הוּא יִשְׁבּוֹר עֻלֵּנוּ מֵעַל צַוָּארֵנוּ, וְהוּא יוֹלִיכֵנוּ קוֹמְמִיּוּת לְאַרְצֵנוּ.

May the Merciful One bless this house and the table on which we ate.

הָרַחֲמָן, הוּא יִשְׁלַח לָנוּ בְּרָכָה מְרֻבָּה בַּבַּיִת הַזֶּה, וְעַל שֻׁלְחָן זֶה שֶׁאָכַלְנוּ עָלָיו.

May the Merciful One send Elijah the prophet to bring good tidings.

הָרַחֲמָן, הוּא יִשְׁלַח לָנוּ אֶת אֵלִיָּהוּ הַנָּבִיא, זָכוּר לַטּוֹב, וִיבַשֶּׂר לָנוּ בְּשׂוֹרוֹת טוֹבוֹת, יְשׁוּעוֹת וְנֶחָמוֹת.

May the Merciful One bless the master of this house and the mistress of this house, and all their dear ones.

הָרַחֲמָן, הוּא יְבָרֵךְ אֶת בַּעַל הַבַּיִת הַזֶּה, וְאֶת אִשְׁתּוֹ, בַּעֲלַת הַבַּיִת הַזֶּה, אוֹתָם וְאֶת בֵּיתָם וְאֶת זַרְעָם, וְאֶת כָּל אֲשֶׁר לָהֶם.

May He bless us and all that is ours with the blessings that He conferred upon our fathers Abraham, Isaac, and Jacob. And let us say, Amen.[22]

אוֹתָנוּ וְאֶת כָּל אֲשֶׁר לָנוּ. כְּמוֹ שֶׁנִּתְבָּרְכוּ אֲבוֹתֵינוּ, אַבְרָהָם יִצְחָק וְיַעֲקֹב בַּכֹּל מִכֹּל כֹּל, כֵּן יְבָרֵךְ אוֹתָנוּ, כֻּלָּנוּ יַחַד, בִּבְרָכָה שְׁלֵמָה, וְנֹאמַר אָמֵן.

May those in heaven pray for us and grant us peace. May we be blessed from God and enjoy the respect of our fellow man.

בַּמָּרוֹם יְלַמְּדוּ עֲלֵיהֶם וְעָלֵינוּ זְכוּת, שֶׁתְּהֵא לְמִשְׁמֶרֶת שָׁלוֹם: וְנִשָּׂא בְרָכָה מֵאֵת יְיָ וּצְדָקָה מֵאֱלֹהֵי יִשְׁעֵנוּ: וְנִמְצָא חֵן וְשֵׂכֶל טוֹב בְּעֵינֵי אֱלֹהִים וְאָדָם.

The following prayers are said at Grace on the celebration of a Brith Milah:

May the Merciful One bless the father and mother of this child; and may they be privileged to rear him wisely. May the *Brith Milah* protect him, and may God watch over him.

הָרַחֲמָן, הוּא יְבָרֵךְ אֲבִי הַיֶּלֶד וְאִמּוֹ, וְיִזְכּוּ לְגַדְּלוֹ וּלְחַנְּכוֹ וּלְחַכְּמוֹ; מִיּוֹם הַשְּׁמִינִי וָהָלְאָה יֵרָצֶה דָמוֹ, וִיהִי יְיָ אֱלֹהָיו עִמּוֹ.

May the Merciful One bless the *sandek* who fulfilled the good deed joyously. May he be rewarded with Your choicest blessings.

הָרַחֲמָן, הוּא יְבָרֵךְ בַּעַל בְּרִית הַמִּילָה, אֲשֶׁר שָׂשׂ לַעֲשׂוֹת צֶדֶק בְּגִילָה; וִישַׁלֵּם פָּעֳלוֹ וּמַשְׂכֻּרְתּוֹ כְּפוּלָה, וְיִתְּנֵהוּ לְמַעְלָה לְמָעְלָה.

May the Merciful One bless the tender infant; that he be loyal to God. May he be privileged to make a pilgrimage to Jerusalem thrice annually.

הָרַחֲמָן, הוּא יְבָרֵךְ רַךְ הַנִּמּוֹל לִשְׁמוֹנָה, וְיִהְיוּ יָדָיו וְלִבּוֹ לְאֵל אֱמוּנָה; וְיִזְכֶּה לִרְאוֹת פְּנֵי הַשְּׁכִינָה, שָׁלֹשׁ פְּעָמִים בַּשָּׁנָה.

May the Merciful One bless the *mohel,* who performed the *mitzvah* properly. One who is faint-hearted may not be a *mohel.*

הָרַחֲמָן, הוּא יְבָרֵךְ הַמָּל בְּשַׂר הָעָרְלָה וּפָרַע וּמָצַץ דְּמֵי הַמִּילָה; אִישׁ הַיָּרֵא וְרַךְ הַלֵּבָב עֲבוֹדָתוֹ פְּסוּלָה, אִם שְׁלָשׁ־אֵלֶּה לֹא יַעֲשֶׂה לָּהּ.

May the Merciful One send us the Messiah, for the sake of our children, to bring good tidings to our dispersed brethren.

הָרַחֲמָן, הוּא יִשְׁלַח לָנוּ מְשִׁיחוֹ הוֹלֵךְ תָּמִים, בִּזְכוּת חַתְנֵי מוּלוֹת דָּמִים; לְבַשֵּׂר בְּשׂוֹרוֹת טוֹבוֹת וְנִחוּמִים, לְעַם אֶחָד מְפֻזָּר וּמְפֹרָד בֵּין הָעַמִּים.

May the Merciful One send Elijah, who remains concealed until the appointed time. He wrapped his face in his mantle when God established His covenant for life and peace.[23]

הָרַחֲמָן, הוּא יִשְׁלַח לָנוּ כֹּהֵן צֶדֶק אֲשֶׁר לֻקַּח לְעֵילוֹם, עַד הוּכַן כִּסְאוֹ כַּשֶּׁמֶשׁ וְיָהֲלוֹם; וַיָּלֶט פָּנָיו בְּאַדַּרְתּוֹ וַיִּגְלוֹם, בְּרִיתִי הָיְתָה אִתּוֹ הַחַיִּים וְהַשָּׁלוֹם.

Continue at Brith Milah and Pidyon Haben, when it is appropriate.

On Sabbath:

May the Merciful One grant us eternal peace in the World-to-Come.[24]

הָרַחֲמָן, הוּא יַנְחִילֵנוּ יוֹם שֶׁכֻּלּוֹ שַׁבָּת וּמְנוּחָה לְחַיֵּי הָעוֹלָמִים.

On Rosh Chodesh:

May the Merciful One grant us a blessed month.

הָרַחֲמָן, הוּא יְחַדֵּשׁ עָלֵינוּ אֶת הַחֹדֶשׁ הַזֶּה לְטוֹבָה וְלִבְרָכָה.

On Festivals:

May the Merciful One grant us a day of unmarried happiness.

הָרַחֲמָן, הוּא יַנְחִילֵנוּ יוֹם שֶׁכֻּלּוֹ טוֹב.

On Rosh Hashanah:

May the Merciful One usher in for us a good and blessed year.

הָרַחֲמָן, הוּא יְחַדֵּשׁ עָלֵינוּ אֶת הַשָּׁנָה הַזֹּאת לְטוֹבָה וְלִבְרָכָה.

On Sukkoth:

May the Merciful One restore the destroyed Tabernacle of David.[25]

הָרַחֲמָן, הוּא יָקִים לָנוּ אֶת סֻכַּת דָּוִד הַנּוֹפָלֶת.

May the Merciful One speedily establish the Messianic Era and the peace of the World-to-Come.

He is merciful to David, His anointed one, and to his dynasty forever.[26]

He who creates harmony in the universe will create peace for us and for the house of David. Amen.

Fear the Lord, all you holy people; for those who fear Him suffer no want. Young lions may go hungry; but the faithful are never lacking for sustenance. Praise the Lord, for He is good; His mercy is eternal. You open Your hand to satisfy everyone's needs. Blessed is the man who relies on the Lord.

I was young and I have grown older, and I have never seen a righteous man abandoned, nor his children begging for food. The Lord will give strength to His people; the Lord will bless His people with peace.[27]

הָרַחֲמָן, הוּא יְזַכֵּנוּ לִימוֹת הַמָּשִׁיחַ וּלְחַיֵּי הָעוֹלָם הַבָּא. מַגְדִּיל (on days when *Musaf* is recited: מִגְדּוֹל) יְשׁוּעוֹת מַלְכּוֹ, וְעֹשֶׂה חֶסֶד לִמְשִׁיחוֹ, לְדָוִד וּלְזַרְעוֹ עַד עוֹלָם. עֹשֶׂה שָׁלוֹם בִּמְרוֹמָיו, הוּא יַעֲשֶׂה שָׁלוֹם עָלֵינוּ וְעַל כָּל יִשְׂרָאֵל, וְאִמְרוּ אָמֵן.

יְראוּ אֶת יְיָ, קְדוֹשָׁיו, כִּי אֵין מַחְסוֹר לִירֵאָיו. כְּפִירִים רָשׁוּ וְרָעֵבוּ, וְדֹרְשֵׁי יְיָ לֹא יַחְסְרוּ כָל טוֹב. הוֹדוּ לַייָ כִּי טוֹב, כִּי לְעוֹלָם חַסְדּוֹ. פּוֹתֵחַ אֶת יָדֶךָ, וּמַשְׂבִּיעַ לְכָל חַי רָצוֹן. בָּרוּךְ הַגֶּבֶר אֲשֶׁר יִבְטַח בַּייָ, וְהָיָה יְיָ מִבְטַחוֹ. נַעַר הָיִיתִי גַּם זָקַנְתִּי, וְלֹא רָאִיתִי צַדִּיק נֶעֱזָב, וְזַרְעוֹ מְבַקֶּשׁ לָחֶם. יְיָ עֹז לְעַמּוֹ יִתֵּן; יְיָ יְבָרֵךְ אֶת עַמּוֹ בַשָּׁלוֹם.

At the conclusion of the Grace, the leader lifts the goblet and recites the blessing for wine:[28]

Blessed are You, Lord our God, King of the universe, who creates the fruit of the vine.[29]

בָּרוּךְ אַתָּה יְיָ אֱלֹהֵינוּ מֶלֶךְ הָעוֹלָם, בּוֹרֵא פְּרִי הַגָּפֶן.

12

The Service at the Circumcision of a Proselyte
סֵדֶר הַבְּרָכוֹת לְמִילַת גֵּרִים

Before circumcising:

anctified us by Your com-
mandments, and commanded
us to circumcise the proselytes.[1]

בָּרוּךְ אַתָּה יְיָ אֱלֹהֵינוּ מֶלֶךְ הָעוֹלָם
אֲשֶׁר קִדְּשָׁנוּ בְּמִצְוֹתָיו וְצִוָּנוּ לָמוּל
אֶת הַגֵּרִים.

After circumcising:

Blessed are You, Lord our
God, King of the universe, who
creates the fruit of the vine.

בָּרוּךְ אַתָּה יְיָ אֱלֹהֵינוּ מֶלֶךְ הָעוֹלָם,
בּוֹרֵא פְּרִי הַגָּפֶן.

Blessed are You, Lord our
God, King of the universe, who
sanctified us with Your commandments, and commanded
us to circumcise the proselytes
and draw the blood of the
covenant. Heaven and earth
cannot exist without the covenant. It is written: "Were it not
for the covenant, there would
not be day or night, heaven or

בָּרוּךְ אַתָּה יְיָ אֱלֹהֵינוּ מֶלֶךְ הָעוֹלָם
אֲשֶׁר קִדְּשָׁנוּ בְּמִצְוֹתָיו וְצִוָּנוּ לָמוּל
אֶת הַגֵּרִים וּלְהַטִּיף מֵהֶם דַּם בְּרִית,
שֶׁאִלְמָלֵא דַם בְּרִית, לֹא נִתְקַיְימוּ
שָׁמַיִם וָאָרֶץ. שֶׁנֶּאֱמַר: אִם לֹא
בְרִיתִי יוֹמָם וָלָיְלָה, חֻקּוֹת שָׁמַיִם
וָאָרֶץ לֹא שָׂמְתִּי. בָּרוּךְ אַתָּה יְיָ
כּוֹרֵת הַבְּרִית.

71

earth."[2] Blessed is God, partner
to the covenant.[3]

Our God and God of our
fathers, preserve this man with
Your Torah and command-
ments, and let his name be
called in Israel . . . the son of
Abraham.[4] May he be happy
with the Torah and commandments. "Give thanks to the
Lord, for He is good; His
mercy endures forever."[5] May
. . . the son of Abraham develop
and enter into God's Torah,
commandments and good
deeds.

אֱלֹהֵינוּ וֵאלֹהֵי אֲבוֹתֵינוּ קַיֵּם אֶת
הָאִישׁ הַזֶּה בְּתוֹרַת אֵל וּבְמִצְוֹתָיו,
וְיִקָּרֵא שְׁמוֹ בְּיִשְׂרָאֵל _____ בֶּן
אַבְרָהָם. יִשְׂמַח בַּתּוֹרָה וְיָגֵל
בְּמִצְוֹת. הוֹדוּ לַייָ כִּי טוֹב כִּי
לְעוֹלָם חַסְדּוֹ. _____ זֶה בֶּן
אַבְרָהָם גָּדוֹל יִהְיֶה, כֵּן יִכָּנֵס בְּתוֹרַת
אֵל וּבְמִצְוֹתָיו וּבְמַעֲשִׂים טוֹבִים.

See Chapter 7 for additional information.

Levinthal

829-3000

Rm. 505

———————

Part II
PIDYON HABEN

PIDYON HABEN
Watercolor by Chaim Gross

13

The Redemption of the First-Born

A mother's first-born is to be dedicated to the service of God, in accordance with the verse, "Sanctify the first-born who opens the womb."[1] This sanctification was the result of an historical event. At the time of the Exodus from Egypt, the tenth plague caused the Egyptian first-born to perish, while the Jewish first-born were spared. God, therefore, decreed that the Jewish first-born should be holy to His service. "All first-born sons are Mine since the day I smote the Egyptian first-born. I sanctified the Israelite first-born; both man and beast they shall be Mine."[2]

The first-born sons became the religious leaders of the Jewish people, and each led his family in worship.[3] This was a unique situation in that each family had its own religious functionary.

The religious ministrations of the first-born lasted only a brief period of time. They were relieved of their sacred task when they joined their fellow Jews in worshipping the golden calf. Only the tribe of Levi remained loyal to God and did not worship the idol.[4] As a result of Levi's loyalty, the members of this tribe were appointed the religious leaders in place of the first-born. The tribe of Levi was divided into two families. The sons of Aaron were the *Cohanim,* and the children of Moses were the Levites. The *Cohanim* were the primary functionaries, and they were assisted by the Levites.

THE FIRST PIDYON HABEN

The first transfer of sanctity from the first-born to the *Cohen*

75

was performed in a direct manner. Each first-born son came to Moses with a *Cohen,* and Moses transferred the sanctity of the first-born to the *Cohen.*[5] There were, however, more first-born sons than *Cohanim.* In order to permit the excess first-born sons to be relieved of their sanctity, the ceremony known as *Pidyon Haben* was introduced. The first-born sons were redeemed by giving Moses five shekels,[6] which he in turn gave to Aaron, the High Priest, and to his sons.[7] Since that first transfer of sanctity from the first-born to the *Cohen,* the ceremony evolved where the father of the first-born son gives the five shekels directly to the *Cohen.* This is known as *Pidyon Haben,* or the redemption of the first-born son, and it takes place when the baby is thirty-one days old.[8]

MITZVAH TO REDEEM THE FIRST-BORN

It is a positive commandment to redeem a son who is the first-born of his mother.[9] The redemption is required when both the father and the mother of the infant are Israelites; i.e., when neither is a descendant of a *Cohen* or a *Levi.*[10]

SIGNIFICANCE OF PIDYON HABEN

The first fruit that one realizes after great effort must be offered as a gift to the Eternal. This is true of agriculture, the birth of a domestic animal, and the first son who opens the mother's womb.[11]

Rabbi Samson R. Hirsch explained: "He thereby appointed, in the midst of the family, the first-born as His representative, to be the bearer, cultivator, and defender of His will. . . . The homes of families are to be kept conscious of the holy mission of the nation."[12]

Another scholar observed that the redemption shekels actually belong to God, but He gave them to the *Cohen.* The Lord ordained that the amount to be given to the *Cohen* for the redemption is five shekels.[13]

When the first-born is redeemed, he is relieved of his sanctity and is permitted to do secular things. Until redemption, he is consecrated to the Almighty and all his efforts may be directed only to the sacred. When he is redeemed, he can live a normal life—working, eating, and playing.[14]

14

Which Child Needs Redemption?

Redemption is obligatory when two conditions are met: (1) the son is the first to open the mother's womb;[1] and (2) both parents are Israelites; i.e., neither is the son or daughter of a *Cohen* or a *Levi.*[2] *Cohanim* and *Leviim* are exempt *a fortiori*: since they exempted the first-born Israelites in the wilderness, they themselves are certainly exempt.[3] Following are additional instances when redemption is not required.

DOUBTFUL CASES

Whenever there is a doubt as to whether a child should be redeemed, we do not redeem him, because this might involve the participants in a meaningless ceremony and the name of the Eternal would be uttered in vain.[4]

An androgynous child or a hermaphrodite—one who has both male and female sex organs—is not redeemed, because this child may not be a male.[5] A *tumtum*—a child whose genitalia are not visible because they are covered with a caul (heavy skin)—does not require redemption because we do not know the child's sex.[6]

If a woman miscarried a fetus that lived more than forty days *in utero,* her next, viable child need not be redeemed. If the miscarried fetus was *in utero* forty days or less, and her next pregnancy results in the birth of a male this child is her first-born son, and requires redemption.[7]

79

Obstetricians calculate the duration of pregnancy from the gestational age. They begin the count from the first day of the last menstrual period, which is about two weeks before ovulation and fertilization. When the obstetrician says that the fetus is forty days old, it is actually forty days minus twelve, or only twenty-eight days. Embryologists count the days from conception.[8]

Physicians call the developing infant an embryo until the eighth week after ovulation, or ten weeks after the last menstrual period.

Our sages selected forty days as the determining time because the embryo has, by this time, taken on the semblance of a human being—it has a head, fingers, and toes. Prior to forty days, the embryo does not resemble a human being. Our sages maintain that the discharge must have a human form to be considered the opening of the womb.[9] When the embryo is forty days old it measures from 22 to 24 millimeters (0.88 to 0.96 inches) in length.

When twins are born, the physician and/or midwife can be relied upon to state which infant was delivered first.[10]

WHEN GENEALOGY IS UNCERTAIN

Rabbi Asher A. Greenwald cites the case of a mother who fled to safety as a child during wartime. She remembers her parents and the town of her birth, but she is not certain whether she is Jewish and certainly does not know if her father was a *Cohen* or a *Levi*. Her first-born need not be redeemed.[11] This type of situation was rare in past generations. Today it has become more prevalent. When in doubt, there is no need to have the child redeemed. An alternate procedure is to have the redemption service but to omit the name of God from the blessings.[12]

A PROSELYTE'S FIRST-BORN

The first-born son of a proselyte who converted to Judaism when she was pregnant is subject to redemption.[13] If, however, she converted to Judaism after giving birth to the child, the child need not be redeemed.[14]

DELIVERY BY CAESAREAN SECTION

A first-born who was delivered by Caesarean section does not require redemption because he did not come forth from the womb, and the Torah writes concerning the baby "who opened the womb."[15]

A BABY WHO PASSES AWAY

Should a baby pass away on or before his thirtieth day of life, there is no obligation to redeem him.[16] If the tragedy occurs after thirty days of life, the child is to be redeemed with the recitation of the blessings for the redemption. The blessing "who granted us life" (*She'he'che'yanu*) is omitted, for it is pronounced only on joyous occasions.

15

Who Is Responsible for the Redemption of the First-Born?

THE FATHER

The father of the first-born son has the responsibility to redeem his child.[1] There are instances where the father of the baby is unable or unwilling to have the child redeemed. The procedure in such cases will be discussed below.

THE MOTHER

The author of one work in the Responsa literature points out that the language in the *Shulchan Arukh* is: *ain ha'isha cha-yeveth,* i.e., "the mother is not obligated" to redeem her son; in other words, she is under no obligation but is certainly permitted to fulfill this *mitzvah* if she wants to.[2] This is especially important where the father is derelict in his religious obligations, or where he is unable to fulfill them. Similarly, the mother steps in when the child's father fails to carry out his other obligations, such as arranging the *Brith Milah* or providing for his son's religious and secular education.

The prevailing custom is for the father to delegate the responsibility to his wife in instances when he cannot be home at the proper time for the redemption of the first-born son.[3]

THE GRANDPARENTS

It is perfectly acceptable for the grandparents to assume the responsibility of redeeming their grandchild when the father is unable or unwilling to fulfill the *mitzvah*. The authorities cite additional cases. In one instance a father who had to leave home to satisfy his military obligations asked the grandparents to redeem the child.[4] Other authorities record their decision in the tragic circumstance where the father of the child passed away before the time of redemption or where the father did not want to redeem his child.[5]

THE RABBINIC COURT

It was noted in reference to *Brith Milah* that the rabbinic court (*Beth Din*) of the community is responsible for seeing that all Jewish children are circumcised. This obligation does not appear to hold true in regard to the redemption of the first-born son. There are authorities who rule that a rabbinic court cannot coerce a father to redeem his son and cannot redeem the child when the father fails to do so.[6] Others maintain that a rabbinic court may redeem the child with charity funds when the father fails to redeem him.[7]

A MESSENGER

A father who knows that he cannot be present at the redemption may appoint a messenger to represent him.[8] The messenger acts for the father and pronounces the blessings of the rite.

AN ABSENT FATHER

A father may redeem his child even if he is in a different city. After ascertaining that the child is well, the father alters the text to confirm the fact that there is no baby present at the redemption—only the *Cohen* and the father. The father informs the *Cohen* that he has a son who needs to be redeemed.[9]

SELF-REDEMPTION

In instances where no redemption took place, the individual is obligated to redeem himself.[10] Here again there is a slight alteration of the text.

Should both father and son require redemption, the father has precedence over the son, though both, of course, need to be redeemed.[11]

THE ADOPTED CHILD

A child who is adopted and who is the first-born son of an Israelite mother requires redemption. See Chapter 5.

16

The Time for the Redemption

The redemption of the first-born is valid only after the infant has attained thirty days of life.[1] It is written, "And God said to Moses: 'Count the first-born males of the children of Israel from one month old and upward.'"[2] The purpose of waiting thirty days is because only then can we be certain that the child is not the result of an untimely birth.[3] The prescribed time to redeem the child is immediately after the thirtieth day, that is, on the thirty-first day.[4]

THE LUNAR MONTH

The lunar month is actually less than 30 days; it is slightly more than 29½ days. There is an opinion that 29½ days may be considered the month mentioned in the Torah.[5] The accepted opinion, however, is that we wait the full thirty days and perform the *Pidyon Haben* on the thirty-first day.[6] Furthermore, unlike other *mitzvoth*, which are fulfilled as soon as possible, the redemption is generally held late in the afternoon. We select a time that will be proper for every child. When the redemption takes place late in the day, we are certain that the full thirty days have elapsed and that we are now in the thirty-first day.[7]

POSTPONEMENT

The Torah does not prescribe the thirty-first day for *Pidyon*

Haben as explicitly as it commands the eighth day for *Brith Milah*. There are postponements that are obligatory; for example, redemption is not performed on a Sabbath or a holiday. This subject will be discussed below. Postponements may not be made for convenience or to enable more people attend the joyous occasion.[8]

When the redemption has been postponed, according to one opinion, it should take place as soon as possible.[9] Another view holds that since it has already been postponed, it may be accomplished whenever it is feasible.[10] The latter view stresses the fact that the Torah states "after" the child is a month old, and the word "after" has no limit in time.

SABBATH, FESTIVALS, AND FAST-DAYS

The redemption of the first-born son should take place when the infant is thirty-one days old. However, if the thirty-first day occurs on a Sabbath or a festival, the redemption is observed on the following day. This is because redemption has elements of a commercial transaction which may not take place on such occasions.[11] It is permissible to have the redemption during the intermediate days of a festival[12] and on Purim.[13]

Should the thirty-first day be a fast-day, the custom is to redeem the child and have the festive meal (*Seudath Mitzvah*) at night prior to the fast-day, provided that the infant is thirty days old at that time.[14]

On Tisha B'Av, when it is forbidden to eat at night as well as the following day, the redemption and the *Seudath Mitzvah* are arranged after the fast is concluded.[15]

REDEMPTION OF AN UNCIRCUMCISED INFANT

An infant who reaches his thirty-first day without being circumcised, due to ill health, may be redeemed. If he is well enough for circumcision on the thirty-first day, the *Brith Milah* is performed first and the redemption may take place that very day.[16]

FIRST-BORN SON ON PASSOVER EVE

First-born sons are under an obligation to fast on the eve of Passover as a means of expressing gratitude that the Jewish first-born sons were spared when the Angel of Death visited the first-born in Egypt. The requirement of fasting on that day is lifted, however, through the custom of participating in a *Seudath Mitzvah* upon the completion of a tractate of Talmud. The obligation to fast applies to all first-born sons, including *Cohanim* and Levites, who do not require redemption, because they too were spared during the plague of the first-born in Egypt.[17]

SHEKEL
Jerusalem, 66 C.E., silver. Hebrew inscription:
Shekel of Israel.

17

The Shekel

The shekel used for the redemption of the first-born son, as well as for other purposes in Biblical times, was a weight rather than a minted coin. The word *shekel* stems from the root *shkl*, meaning "to weigh." The shekel was used in all Semitic countries, including Eretz Israel. Metal weights equaling a shekel were used to balance items bought in the marketplace or offered for sacred purposes in the Temple in Jerusalem.[1]

The Bible actually refers to three different types of shekel: the merchant's weight (*over la'sokher*),[2] the sanctuary weight (*shekel hakodesh*),[3] and the king's weight (*shekel b'even hamelekh*).[4] The shekel used for the redemption of the first-born was the sanctuary weight.

We will attempt to determine the actual weight of the sanctuary shekel in order to ascertain the amount of silver required to fulfill the obligation of giving the *Cohen* five shekels or *sela'im*.[5]

Our sages disagreed on the weight of the shekel because they encountered two difficulties. Firstly, most of them had never seen a shekel and consequently never had the opportunity to weigh one. Secondly, there was no uniformity of weight in the coins of their own time.[6]

We must overcome these difficulties in order to determine our own religious obligations. In the opinion of Rabbi Meir, even Moses required assistance on this matter. Because Moses was uncertain of the exact weight of the shekel, Rabbi Meir said, "The Almighty took a fiery shekel from beneath the Throne of Glory and showed it to Moses, saying, 'This is the amount that shall be given to the Sanctuary.'"[7] Centuries later, Rabbi Moses Maimonides wrote, "I received the tradition from my father, of blessed memory, and he in turn received the tradition from his father, that the sanctuary shekel weighed the same as 384 barley seeds."[8]

GRAIN WEIGHT

Weighing items by grains of seed has continued to this day. The only difference is that currently the "grain" refers to wheat seed rather than barley seed.[9] The term "gram" is from the Latin *granum,* or "grain," and it refers to the number of grains of seed in a gram.[10] It has been established that there were 22.2 barley seeds in a gram.[11]

Silver and gold are measured by the troy ounce rather than the avoirdupois ounce that we customarily employ.[12]

ARCHAEOLOGICAL DISCOVERIES

Archaeologists have uncovered dome-shaped metals dating back to the seventh century B.C.E. Some of these specify their weight; i.e., a shekel or a fraction thereof.[13] They range in weight from 2.49 to 2.63 grams and are inscribed "one quarter-shekel."[14] Fortunately, silver shekels have been found as well.[15] These date from the Jewish war against Rome (66–70 C.E.) and bear the inscription in Hebrew "Shekel of Israel." On the reverse side of the coin there is a stem of fruit (probably a pomegranate) encircled by the words "Jerusalem is holy" inscribed in Hebrew. These silver sanctuary shekels range in weight from 14.1 to 14.52 grams.

RABBINIC COMPUTATIONS

Rashi (1040–1105) maintained that the shekel was half the weight of an *uncia,* or half an ounce by the standard weight of Cologne.[16] He designated the *uncia* from the city of Cologne because, during his time and for centuries thereafter, there were four different weights for the ounce in Europe.[17] The *uncia* mentioned by Rashi consisted of 29.92 grams. Half this amount is 14.96. His computation is almost identical in weight to the silver sanctuary shekels that were found by the archaeologists. In Rashi's opinion, the five shekels needed for the redemption would be 5 x 14.96, or 74.80 grams of silver.

Maimonides, as noted above, measured the shekel by the weight of 384 barley seeds. When we divide this number by 22.2 seeds to the gram, we arrive at his conclusion that a shekel weighed 17.29 grams.

Nachmanides (Ramban) disagreed with Rashi and maintained that the shekel was three-quarters of an *uncia*.[18] We are not certain which *uncia* he had in mind, but we do know his conclusion, that a sanctuary shekel weighed 17.40 grams.[19] Nachmanides was, therefore, very close to the opinion of Maimonides.

Nachmanides went on *aliyah* in 1267 c.e. and arrived at the port of Acco.[20] Shortly after his arrival, the elders of the community showed him a sanctuary shekel. Nachmanides had the coin weighed, and the result convinced him that Rashi was indeed correct. He issued a letter stating his corrected position.[21]

THE ESTABLISHED PRACTICE

During the last two centuries our sages ruled that additional grams were needed to accommodate the fact that barley seeds are now slightly heavier than they were during the time of the early scholars (*Rishonim*).[22] Since the sages were not willing to forsake the tradition that Maimonides had received, they reevaluated the barley seeds in accordance with their current weight.

The generally accepted view is that 96 grams of silver are required for the redemption. This may be converted to 3.087 troy ounces of silver.[23]

The United States silver dollar, minted from 1840 to 1935, consists of 0.7734 troy ounces of silver and has a fineness of .800. We use five silver dollars, which total 3.667 troy ounces of silver.

Silver coins from other countries can be similarly evaluated.

One must ascertain the silver content and the fineness.[24] Thus the Canadian silver dollar, minted from 1935 to 1967, has a silver content of 0.600 troy ounces and a fineness of .800. Six Canadian silver dollars are thus required for the redemption.

Only four British crowns, minted from 1816 to 1919, are needed because each consists of 0.8409 troy ounces and has a fineness of .925. The crown is not easily attainable. Consequently, the Rabbinate in Britain allows the use of the shilling, of which thirty are needed for the redemption.[25]

MISCELLANEOUS VALUES AND USAGES OF THE SHEKEL

Our father Abraham bought the cave in Machpelah in Hebron, as the final resting place for his wife Sarah, for 400 shekels of silver.[26] The shekel in Abraham's day was a unit of weight equal to 8.4 grams based on the Babylonian shekel, which was called *šiqlu.*[27]

In the wedding agreement the word *zakuk* is used instead of shekel. Chazon Ish maintains that each piece of silver which is called *zakuk* is the equivalent of 15 shekels.[28] Thus, when the bridegroom obligates himself to 200 silver pieces, it means 200 x 15, or 3,000 shekels.

There is a custom to donate one half of the standard coin of the realm before reading the Book of Esther, the Purim *Megillah.* Its purpose is to remember the half-shekel that was given during the month of Adar for the maintenance of the Temple worship. In some communities the funds are distributed to the needy, and in others they are given to the individual who reads the *Megillah.*[29]

The shekel was used during the early days of the Zionist movement. The purchasers of the shekel became members of the Zionist quest for a Jewish homeland and were qualified to vote for the delegates to the Zionist Congress.[30]

The government of Israel issued a *Pidyon Haben* set in 1970. Its purpose was to make available to parents five coins that would have the proper amount of silver content for the redemption of their sons. The issuance of this set was discontinued in 1977.

In honor of Chanukah 1980, the Israeli government issued the first silver shekels since the last minting, nineteen centuries ago. Israel's shekel of modern times is identical in metal fineness and weight to the ancient one. It is sculpted of silver with a fineness of .850 and weighs 14.4 grams. It depicts the Chanukah *Menorah* in use on the island of Corfu, off the coast of Greece, where a Jewish community of over 500 families perished in the Holocaust.

18

The Cohen

The overwhelming majority of people who consider themselves to be *Cohanim,* descendants of the ancient priestly tribe, do not have conclusive proof to that effect. We accept a person's statement that his father was a *Cohen* and, therefore, that he too is a *Cohen.*[1]

QUALIFICATIONS

The redemption is conducted with an adult *Cohen.*[2] The parents should select a *Cohen* who is a Torah scholar and/or one who is impoverished, and thus they can fulfill the good deed of helping the needy, whenever possible.[3] The Talmud states that parents should avoid having the redemption accomplished with a person who does not observe and revere the Torah.[4] It is permissible to delay the redemption for several days in order to obtain a suitable *Cohen.*[5] When a proper *Cohen* cannot be found, it is permissible to have a *Cohen* with less than the optimal qualifications.[6]

WHEN NO COHEN IS AVAILABLE

There are two options when there is no *Cohen* in the community: (1) an Israelite may serve as the messenger (*shaliach*) for the *Cohen,*[7] or (2) the daughter of a *Cohen* may accept the redemption, but then the blessings should be omitted.[8] Should a *Cohen* become available, the redemption may be repeated with the blessings.

MONEY OR ITS EQUIVALENT

The five shekels or *sela'im* may be given in coins or with an object that is worth the required amount.[9] Paper money may not be used because it is considered to be a note of indebtedness on the part of the government.[10]

Should the item given the *Cohen* be worth less than the prescribed amount, the father may simply add the needed money so that the total will equal five shekels. There are authorities who rule that if the *Cohen* accepts the item, even though it is worth less than five shekels, he shows that it has the proper value for him, and the father need not give additional money.[11]

THE COHEN MAY RETURN THE FIVE SHEKELS

The *Cohen* may accept the five shekels as the redemption for the first-born and subsequently return the sum to the father.[12] The father, however, may not give the money on condition that it be returned. There are authorities who maintain that the money may not be returned except in instances where the family is impoverished and cannot afford the expenditure.[13]

In view of the fact that five silver dollars may not always be readily available, because the government has stopped minting these coins, it is recommended that a *Cohen* who is frequently called upon to redeem children have on hand suitable coins which he can sell to the father, who can then use them for the redemption.[14]

WHEN THE COHEN IS IN MOURNING

The fact that the *Cohen* is in mourning is no deterrent. He may officiate at the redemption even during the time preceding the burial of his kinfolk. He may perform the redemption because the *mitzvah* is not the obligation of the *Cohen* but of the family of the child. The blessing for the wine, however, is recited by another person attending the redemption service.[15] A father who is in mourning, too, may redeem his child.[16]

PIDYON HABEN PLATE
Brass: repoussé and engraved; 2¼ × 18½ dm.

19

Comments on the Redemption of the First-Born Son

The first-born were sanctified shortly before our ancestors were liberated from Egyptian bondage. The Torah defines this sanctification with the word *v'ha'a'varta,* "You shall *set apart* to the Lord all who open the womb."[1] In other words, the first-born sons are consecrated to the service of the Lord and are forbidden to occupy themselves with the secular and the worldly. The Torah, however, provided us with a procedure to lift this sanctity—the redemption of the first-born by the *Cohen.*

This is the implied question that the *Cohen* asks the parents of the holy child: "Which do you prefer—that your first-born son remain completely set apart and sacred unto the Lord, or do you wish to redeem him from his sanctity with five shekels?"[2] The answer of the parents can be readily anticipated. They would prefer that the child be able to live normally, like all other children, occupying himself with the usual activities as well as devoting part of his time and effort to the sacred. There are very few parents who would want their child to be totally and completely consecrated to the service of the Almighty. When parents comprehend the difference between a redeemed and an unredeemed child, they will want to have the child redeemed and released from his sanctity.[3]

QUORUM

The service of redemption for the first-born son does not

require the presence of a quorum (*minyan*). When it is not possible or feasible to have an elaborate ceremony, a very simple one will satisfy the religious requirements. The service of redemption may take place with only the parents, the infant, and the *Cohen*.[4]

SEUDATH MITZVAH

It is a meritorious deed to have a quorum and a meal at the redemption of the first-born son.[5] The repast, no matter how modest, is considered to be a festive meal (*Seudath Mitzvah*).[6] These customs have been observed since the time of the Talmud (500 C.E.).[7]

All who are present at the redemption wash their hands and recite the blessing "concerning the washing of the hands" (*al netilath yadayim*), which is followed by the blessing for bread (*ha-motzi lechem min ha'aretz*).[8]

The *Cohen* should have previously made certain that the infant is the mother's first-born and that she did not have a miscarriage prior to the birth of this child.[9]

The child is brought in, dressed in festive attire, on an embellished silver tray.

The baby's father recites the accepted formula in behalf of his wife and himself. "This child is the first-born of his mother, and the Holy One, praised be He, has commanded that he be redeemed; as it is written: 'And the redemption, from a month old shall you redeem him, shall be, five shekels of silver, after the shekel of the Sanctuary—which is twenty gerahs' (Numbers 18:16). And it is said again, 'Sanctify unto Me all the first-born, who open the womb among the children of Israel, of both man and beast shall be Mine'" (Exodus 13:2).[10]

The *Cohen* then asks the father, "Which do you prefer, to give me your first-born, or to redeem him for five *sela'im* which you are obliged according to the Torah?" The father replies, "I prefer to redeem my son, and here is the redemption, as I am obliged by the Torah."

The father recites the benediction for the redemption and

"Who granted us life" (*She'he'che'yanu*). Following these bless-ings the father gives the *Cohen* five shekels.[11]

"WHO GRANTED US LIFE"

The blessing "Who granted us life" (*She'he'che'yanu*) thanks the Lord for granting us life and permitting us to enjoy a happy occasion. The father utters this blessing at the redemption service because it commemorates a *mitzvah* which is accompanied by a joyous celebration.[12]

A father who redeemed a child with his first wife may recite this blessing again if he remarries and his second wife has a first-born son.[13]

The blessing may be said when the father is in mourning and during the time of community mourning, from the seventeenth of Tammuz through the ninth of Av (*Bain Hamtzarim*).[14]

THE COHEN

After the father has said the two blessings, he hands the five shekels to the *Cohen*. The latter holds the redemption money over the child's head and says, "This money is in place of the child, this is in his exchange and the money is for the redemption of the infant."[15]

The *Cohen* places his hands on the baby's head and blesses him.[16] The family's rabbi should offer a blessing as well.[17] Follow-ing the blessing for the welfare of the child, the *Cohen* intones the blessing for wine to signal the fact that he has fulfilled the com-mandment to redeem the child.[18] Sephardim in Jerusalem add the blessing for the aroma of spice.[19]

ARAMAIC

The *Cohen*'s question and the father's response are uttered in the Aramaic language. This is because these texts are from the Gaonic period (589–1038 C.E.), when the Jewish people lived in

Babylonia and their spoken language was Aramaic.[20] The dialogue between the *Cohen* and father may be recited in whatever language is best understood.[21] Should the father be unable to read the Aramaic and Hebrew portions, it has been suggested that he be taught to do so.[22] Transliterations are presented in Chapter 21.

TEXTS FOR DIFFERENT CIRCUMSTANCES

There are times when the circumstances of the redemption differ from the norm. The usual situation is when the parents, the child, and the *Cohen* are present. Sometimes, however, the father is away, and he arranges the redemption without the child being present. Then, there is the instance where the father is away and he delegates a messenger to fulfill the redemption for him. Finally, there is the situation where a person who was not redeemed by his parents approaches the *Cohen* and asks to be redeemed.[23] The Sephardic rite will also be offered.[24]

GRACE ON CONCLUDING THE FESTIVE MEAL

Where there is a *Seudath Mitzvah* in conjunction with the *Pidyon Haben,* Grace After the Meal should be said. See Chapter 11.

20

Texts on the Redemption of the First-Born

BIBLE

God said to Moses, "Sanctify every first-born who opens the womb among the Israelites, both man and beasts, it is Mine."[1]

You must redeem every first-born son.[2]

Do not delay the offerings of your harvest and presses; give Me your first-born.[3]

You shall redeem every first-born son. Do not appear before Me empty-handed.[4]

God said to Moses, "I separated the Levites from their brethren so that they may take the place of all the first-born who open the womb among the Israelites. All first-born are Mine since the day I smote the Egyptian first-born. I sanctified the Israelite first-born, both man and beast shall be Mine."[5]

God said to Moses, "Count the first-born Israelites who are one month old and upward, and make a census of their names. And you shall take the Levites for Me—I am God—instead of the first-born Israelites. And take the Levites' cattle instead of the Israelites' first-born cattle."

Moses counted the first-born Israelites, as God commanded him. The first-born Israelites who were one month and older numbered 22,273, according to the number of their names. God spoke to Moses, "Take the Levites instead of all the first-born Israelites; and the Levites' cattle instead of [the Israelites' first-born] cattle. The Levites shall be Mine I am God. And for the redemption of the 273 first-born who outnumber the Levites; you shall take five sanctuary shekels—the shekel is twenty gerahs. Give the silver to Aaron and his sons as a redemption for [the first-born who are] in excess [of the Levites]." Moses took the redemption money for the first-born who outnumbered the Levites. The silver that he took from the first-born Israelites was 1,365 sanctuary shekels. Moses gave the silver for those who were redeemed to Aaron and his sons at God's command.[6]

The [Levites] are given to Me instead of the first-born of all the Israelites. I have taken them for Myself. This is because all first-born of the Israelites are Mine, man and beast alike. I sanctified them for Myself on that day that I killed all the first-born in Egypt. I have now taken the Levites instead of all the first-born Israelites.[7]

The redemption [of a first-born son] from one month old shall be fixed at five sanctuary shekels—the shekel is twenty gerahs.[8]

TEACHINGS OF THE RABBIS

Rabbi Joshua the son of Levi said, "In twenty-four places *Cohanim* are called Levites. The following instance is one of them: 'But the *Cohanim* the Levites the sons of Zadok.'"[9]

The Rabbis offered the following commentary to the verse: "You shall take five sanctuary shekels [for the redemption of the first-born]."

Moses reasoned, "If I say to a man, 'Give me the shekels for your redemption,' he might answer, 'A Levite has already redeemed me.'" So what did Moses do? He brought twenty-two thousand slips and wrote on each, "Levite," and on another two hundred and seventy-three he wrote, "five shekels." Then he put them into an urn and mixed them up and said to the people, "Draw your slips." To each who drew a slip with the word "Levite," he said, "a Levite has redeemed you." To each who drew a slip with "five shekels" on it, he said, "Pay your redemption."[10]

Before the Sanctuary was erected, the high places (*bamoth*) were permitted and the service was performed by the first-born; after the Sanctuary was set up, high places were forbidden and the service was performed by *Cohanim.*[11]

Rabbi Johanan said, "The first-born were sanctified and their holiness continues for all time."[12]

A father has the following obligations to his son: to circumcise him, to redeem the first-born, to teach him Torah, to provide him with a wife, and to teach him a craft. Some say, to teach him to swim.[13]

Our Rabbis taught: there are three partners in man: the Holy One, blessed be He, the father, and the mother.[14]

The transfer of sanctity from the first-born to the *Cohen* was valid only in the wilderness. Henceforth, the redemption will be accomplished with the redemption of the first-born.[15]

The redemption is performed with male *Cohanim,* as it is written, "Give the silver to Aaron and his sons."[16]

The service was performed by the first-born. When they sinned with the golden calf they were relieved of this sacred task. The Levites, who had abstained from the idolatrous worship, were selected to replace the first-born.[17]

The twenty gerahs, or five shekels, are to remind us that Joseph, Rachel's first-born, was sold for twenty pieces of silver.[18]

An Israelite who is blessed with a first-born son is obligated to sanctify the child for the service of God, as it is written: "Sanctify to Me every first-born who opens the womb among the Israelites."[19]

We are commanded to sanctify the first-born, that is, to set the child apart from all secular activities.[20]

The son must fulfill all the obligations, if the father failed to do them.[21]

The Holy One, blessed be He, does not elevate a person to leadership until he determines that he is worthy. The tribe of Levi remained loyal to God during the servitude in Egypt. They did not worship idols and they circumcised their sons. Similarly, when the Israelites worshiped the golden calf in the wilderness, the Levites refrained. That is why God selected the tribe of Levi—the Levites and the *Cohanim*—to serve Him.[22]

The first-born is ascribed to the mother, not the father, because she knows who is the first-born, and because she has more compassion for the infant than does the father.[23]

REASONS FOR THE REDEMPTION OF THE FIRST-BORN

It was the practice of the pagans to offer their first-born sons as human sacrifices to their pagan god (*molekh*). Therefore, the Almighty commanded that the Jewish first-born be elevated to sanctity, not sacrifice.[24]

Rabbi Nehemiah said, "The Holy One, blessed be He, told Israel: 'When you enter the land of Israel, you must set apart unto Me all that opens the womb.' This is because He had compassion on them in Egypt. It can be compared to a king who made a banquet for his daughter on her release after she was imprisoned by enemies. God, too, performed miracles for Israel, slaying the first-born of the Egyptians on their account. Therefore, He exhorted them concerning the sanctity of the first-born."[25]

Another reason is that we remember that everything in creation belongs to God. And all our possessions are gifts from the Almighty to His creatures. Consequently, we offer the first fruits to Him.[26]

He [the Eternal] thereby appointed, in the midst of the family, the first-born as His representative, to be the bearer, cultivator, and defender of His will. . . . the homes and families are to be conscious of the holy mission of the nation, that in every home and family it is only the great national calling that becomes developed in the whole manifold diversity of the characteristics of families and homes.[27]

The redemption is actually from God. But He gave the redemption to the *Cohen.*[28]

21

Redemption Rites of the First-Born Son
סֵדֶר פִּדְיוֹן הַבֵּן

THE ASHKENAZIC RITE

The parents carry the infant on a tray and present him to the Cohen. All assembled wash their hands and pronounce this blessing.

Blessed are You, Lord our God, King of the universe, who sanctified us with Your commandments, and commanded us concerning the washing of the hands.

בָּרוּךְ אַתָּה יְיָ אֱלֹהֵינוּ מֶלֶךְ הָעוֹלָם. אֲשֶׁר קִדְּשָׁנוּ בְּמִצְוֹתָיו וְצִוָּנוּ עַל נְטִילַת יָדָיִם.

The assembled then say the blessing over the bread.[1]

Blessed are You, Lord our God, King of the universe, who brings forth bread from the earth.

בָּרוּךְ אַתָּה יְיָ אֱלֹהֵינוּ מֶלֶךְ הָעוֹלָם הַמּוֹצִיא לֶחֶם מִן הָאָרֶץ.

The father of the child says:

זֶה בְּנִי בְכוֹרִי הוּא פֶּטֶר רֶחֶם לְאִמּוֹ, וְהַקָּדוֹשׁ בָּרוּךְ הוּא צִוָּה הוּא לִפְדוֹתוֹ, שֶׁנֶּאֱמַר: וּפְדוּיָו מִבֶּן חֹדֶשׁ תִּפְדֶּה בְּעֶרְכְּךָ כֶּסֶף חֲמֵשֶׁת שְׁקָלִים, בְּשֶׁקֶל הַקֹּדֶשׁ, עֶשְׂרִים גֵּרָה הוּא. וְנֶאֱמַר: קַדֶּשׁ־לִי כָל בְּכוֹר; פֶּטֶר כָּל רֶחֶם בִּבְנֵי יִשְׂרָאֵל, בָּאָדָם וּבַבְּהֵמָה, לִי הוּא.

111

Zeh b'ni b'khori hu peter rechem l'imo, v'Hakadosh ba-rukh Hu tziva lifdotho, she-ne-'e'mar: "Ufduyav miben cho-desh tifdeh b'er'k'kha kesef chamaisheth sh'kalim, b'shekel hakodesh — esrim gerah hu." V'ne'e'mar: "Kadaish Li khal b'khor, peter kal rechem bivnai Yisrael, ba'adam u'vabhaima Li hu."

This child is his mother's first-born. And the Holy One, blessed be He, commanded that he be redeemed, as it is written: "The redemption of the first-born, when he is one month old, shall be five shekels, after the sanctuary shekel, or twenty gerahs." An additional verse states: "Sanctify the first-born, the first-born in Israel, both man and beast, they are Mine."[2]

The Cohen asks the father:

מַאי בָּעִית טְפֵי לְתֵּן לִי, בִּנְךָ בְּכוֹרְךָ שֶׁהוּא פֶּטֶר רֶחֶם לְאִמּוֹ, אוֹ בָּעִית לִפְדוֹתוֹ בְּעַד חָמֵשׁ סְלָעִים, כִּדְמְחַיַבְתְּ מִדְּאוֹרַיְתָא?

Mai ba'ith t'fai litain li, binkha b'khorkha shehu peter rechem l'imo, o ba'ith lifdotho b'ad chamaish sela'im kid'm'chu-yavt mid'Oraytha?

Do you prefer to give me your son, or would you rather redeem him for five *sela'im*, which you are required to give according to the Torah?[3]

The father responds to the question, gives the Cohen the five shekels, and then offers two blessings:

חָפֵץ אֲנִי לִפְדּוֹת אֶת בְּנִי, וְהֵילָךְ דְּמֵי פִדְיוֹנוֹ, כִּדְמְחַיַבְתִּי מִדְּאוֹרַיְתָא.
בָּרוּךְ אַתָּה יְיָ אֱלֹהֵינוּ מֶלֶךְ הָעוֹלָם, אֲשֶׁר קִדְּשָׁנוּ בְּמִצְוֹתָיו וְצִוָּנוּ עַל פִּדְיוֹן הַבֵּן.

בָּרוּךְ אַתָּה יְיָ אֱלֹהֵינוּ מֶלֶךְ הָעוֹלָם, שֶׁהֶחֱיָנוּ וְקִיְּמָנוּ וְהִגִּיעָנוּ, לַזְּמַן הַזֶּה.

Chafaitz ani lif'doth eth b'ni, v'hailakh d'mai fid'yono,

I want to redeem my son, and take the redemption, which I

k'di'm'chu'yavti mid'Orai'tha.

am required to give according to the Torah.[4]

Barukh ata Adonoy, Elohainu Melekh ha'olam, asher kid'-shanu b'mitz'vo'thav v'tzivanu al pidyon haben.

Blessed are You, Lord our God, King of the universe, who sanctified us with Your commandments and commanded us concerning the redemption of the first-born.[5]

Barukh ata Adonoy, Elohainu Melekh ha'olam, she'he'che'-yanu v'kimanu v'higiyanu laz-man hazeh.

Blessed are You, Lord our God, King of the universe, who kept us alive, sustained us, and enabled us to reach this season.[6]

The Cohen holds the redemption over the child's head and says:

זֶה תַּחַת זֶה, זֶה חִלּוּף זֶה, זֶה מָחוּל עַל זֶה; וְיִכָּנֵס זֶה הַבֵּן לְחַיִּים, לְתוֹרָה
וּלְיִרְאַת שָׁמָיִם. יְהִי רָצוֹן, שֶׁכְּשֵׁם שֶׁנִּכְנַס לַפִּדְיוֹן, כֵּן יִכָּנֵס לְתוֹרָה וּלְחֻפָּה
וּלְמַעֲשִׂים טוֹבִים, אָמֵן.

Zeh tachath zeh, zeh chiluf zeh, zeh machul al zeh. V'yikanais zeh haben l'chayim, l'Thorah ul'yirath shamayim. Y'hi ra-tzon, she'k'shaim shenikhnas lapid'yon kain yikanais l'Tho-rah, ul'chupah, ul'ma'asim tovim. Amen.

This is instead of that; this in exchange for that; this is in remission of that. May this child enter into a life of Torah and Godliness. Even as he has been admitted to redemption, so may he enter into Torah, the wedding canopy, and to a life of good deeds. Amen.[7]

The Cohen places his hand on the head of the child and blesses him:

יְשִׂימְךָ אֱלֹהִים כְּאֶפְרַיִם וְכִמְנַשֶּׁה. יְבָרֶכְךָ יְיָ וְיִשְׁמְרֶךָ. יָאֵר יְיָ פָּנָיו אֵלֶיךָ
וִיחֻנֶּךָּ. יִשָּׂא יְיָ פָּנָיו אֵלֶיךָ, וְיָשֵׂם לְךָ שָׁלוֹם.

יְיָ שׁוֹמְרֶךָ, יְיָ צִלְּךָ עַל יַד יְמִינֶךָ. כִּי אֹרֶךְ יָמִים וּשְׁנוֹת חַיִּים וְשָׁלוֹם יוֹסִיפוּ לָךְ. יְיָ יִשְׁמָרְךָ מִכָּל רָע, יִשְׁמוֹר אֶת נַפְשֶׁךָ. אָמֵן.

God make you like Ephraim and Manasseh.[8] The Lord bless you and sustain you; the Lord cause His face to shine on you and be gracious to you; the Lord grant you peace.[9]

The Lord will protect you from all evil; He will always be near you.[10] May you be blessed with a long and happy life. The Lord will guard you from all evil, He will protect your life.[11]

The Cohen lifts the goblet and offers the blessing for wine:

בָּרוּךְ אַתָּה יְיָ אֱלֹהֵינוּ מֶלֶךְ הָעוֹלָם, בּוֹרֵא פְּרִי הַגָּפֶן.

Blessed are You, Lord our God, King of the universe, who creates the fruit of the vine.

The assembled may now enjoy the repast, which is a festive meal (Seudath Mitzvah). At the conclusion Grace after Meals is said (see Chapter 11).

REDEMPTION OF AN ADULT

A first-born (*b'khor*) who was not redeemed is obligated to have himself redeemed. The ritual is the same as with an infant, but the declaration to the *Cohen* and the dialogue between the *Cohen* and the first-born is made to fit the circumstances.[12]

The first-born (b'khor) declares:

אֲנִי בְּכוֹר פֶּטֶר רֶחֶם וְהִנְנִי שֶׁלָּךְ.

Ani b'khor peter rechem v'hi-   I am my mother's first-born
neni shelkha.   son, and I belong to you.

The Cohen asks the first-born:

אַתָּה רוֹצֶה לִהְיוֹת שֶׁלִּי אוֹ לָתֵת לִי ה׳ סְלָעִים שֶׁאַתָּה חַיָּיב לִי בְּפִקְדוֹנְךָ?

Ata rotzeh l'hiyoth sheli o lathaith li hai sela'im she'ata chayav li b'fidyonekha?

Do you prefer to be mine, or would you rather give me the five *sela'im* that you are obligated to give me for your redemption?

The first-born responds:

אֲנִי רוֹצֶה לִפְדּוֹת עַצְמִי וְהֵא לָךְ.

Ani rotzeh lifdoth atzmi v'hai lakh.

I want to redeem myself; please accept the five *sela'im* for my redemption.

The first-born recites the two blessings:

בָּרוּךְ אַתָּה יְיָ אֱלֹהֵינוּ מֶלֶךְ הָעוֹלָם, אֲשֶׁר קִדְּשָׁנוּ בְּמִצְוֹתָיו וְצִוָּנוּ עַל פִּדְיוֹן הַבֵּן.

בָּרוּךְ אַתָּה יְיָ אֱלֹהֵינוּ מֶלֶךְ הָעוֹלָם, שֶׁהֶחֱיָנוּ וְקִיְּמָנוּ וְהִגִּיעָנוּ, לַזְּמַן הַזֶּה.

Barukh ata Adonoy, Elohainu, Melekh ha'olam asher kid'shanu b'mitz'vo'thav v'tzivanu al pidyon haben.

Blessed are You, Lord our God, King of the universe, who sanctified us with Your commandments and commanded us concerning the redemption of the first-born.[13]

Barukh ata Adonoy, Elohainu, Melekh ha'olam she'he'che'yanu v'kimanu v'higiyanu lazman hazeh.

Blessed are You, Lord our God, King of the universe, who kept us alive, sustained us, and enabled us to reach this season.[14]

The Cohen holds the redemption over the first-born's head and says:

זֶה תַּחַת זֶה, זֶה חִלּוּף זֶה, זֶה מָחוּל עַל זֶה; וְיִכָּנֵס זֶה הַבֵּן לְחַיִּים, לְתוֹרָה וּלְיִרְאַת שָׁמָיִם. יְהִי רָצוֹן, שֶׁכְּשֵׁם שֶׁנִּכְנַס לַפִּדְיוֹן, כֵּן יִכָּנֵס לְתוֹרָה וּלְחֻפָּה וּלְמַעֲשִׂים טוֹבִים, אָמֵן.

Zeh tachath zeh, zeh chiluf zeh, zeh machul al zeh. V'yikanais zeh haben l'chayim, l'Thorah ul'yirath shamayim. Y'hi ratzon, she'k'shaim shenikhnas lapid'yon, kain y'kanais l'Thorah, ul'chupah, ul'ma'asim tovim. Amen.

This is instead of that; this in exchange of that. May this son enter into a life of Torah and Godliness. Even as he has been admitted to redemption, so may he enter into Torah, the wedding canopy, and to a life of good deeds. Amen.[15]

The Cohen places his hand on the head of the first-born and blesses him:

יְשִׂימְךָ אֱלֹהִים כְּאֶפְרַיִם וְכִמְנַשֶּׁה. יְבָרֶכְךָ יְיָ וְיִשְׁמְרֶךָ. יָאֵר יְיָ פָּנָיו אֵלֶיךָ וִיחֻנֶּךָּ. יִשָּׂא יְיָ פָּנָיו אֵלֶיךָ, וְיָשֵׂם לְךָ שָׁלוֹם. יְיָ שׁוֹמְרֶךָ, יְיָ צִלְּךָ עַל יַד יְמִינֶךָ. כִּי אֹרֶךְ יָמִים וּשְׁנוֹת חַיִּים וְשָׁלוֹם יוֹסִיפוּ לָךְ. יְיָ יִשְׁמָרְךָ מִכָּל רָע, יִשְׁמֹר אֶת נַפְשֶׁךָ. אָמֵן.

God make you like Ephraim and Manasseh.[16] The Lord bless you and sustain you; the Lord cause His face to shine on you and be gracious to you; the Lord grant you peace.[17]

The Lord will protect you from all evil; He will always be near you.[18] May you be blessed with a long and happy life. The Lord will guard you from all evil, He will protect your life.[19]

The Cohen lifts the goblet and offers the blessing for wine:

בָּרוּךְ אַתָּה יְיָ אֱלֹהֵינוּ מֶלֶךְ הָעוֹלָם, בּוֹרֵא פְּרִי הַגָּפֶן.

Blessed are You, Lord our God, King of the universe, who creates the fruit of the vine.

The assembled may now enjoy the repast, which is a festive meal (Seudath Mitzvah). At the conclusion Grace After Meals is said (see Chapter 11).

EMISSARY OF THE FATHER

Should the father be out of town when his son becomes thirty-one days old and requires redemption, two options are available to him. The father may delegate an emissary to represent him or he may arrange to have the redemption done without the presence of the infant.

If the father chooses to have an emissary, he should authorize him to fulfill all the necessary functions. He must also provide the emissary with the five shekels. The following is the text of the dialogue between the *Cohen* and the father's emissary.[20]

The emissary says:

זֶה הַבֵּן בְּכוֹר הוּא פֶּטֶר רֶחֶם לְאִמּוֹ הַיִשְׂרְאֵלִית, וְהַקָּדוֹשׁ בָּרוּךְ הוּא צִוָּה לִפְדּוֹתוֹ, שֶׁנֶּאֱמַר: וּפְדוּיָו מִבֶּן חֹדֶשׁ תִּפְדֶּה בְּעֶרְכְּךָ כֶּסֶף חֲמֵשֶׁת שְׁקָלִים בְּשֶׁקֶל הַקֹּדֶשׁ עֶשְׂרִים גֵּרָה הוּא. וְנֶאֱמַר: קַדֶּשׁ לִי כָל בְּכוֹר פֶּטֶר כָּל רֶחֶם בִּבְנֵי יִשְׂרָאֵל בָּאָדָם וּבַבְּהֵמָה לִי הוּא. וַאֲנִי שָׁלִיחַ שֶׁל אֲבִי הַיֶּלֶד הַבְּכוֹר הַזֶּה, שֶׁהִגִּיעַ זְמַן פִּדְיוֹנוֹ.

Zeh haben b'khor hu peter rechem l'imo haYisr'ailith, v'Hakadosh barukh Hu tziva lifdotho, she'ne'e'mar: "Ufduyov miben chodesh tifdeh b'er'k'kha kesef chamaisheth sh'kalim b'shekel hakodesh-esrim gerah hu." V'ne'e'mar: "Kadaish Li khal b'khor, peter kol rechem bivnai Yisrael, ba'-adam u'vabhaima Li hu." V'ani sh'liach shel avi hayeled hab'-

This child is his Israelite mother's first-born. And the Holy One, blessed be He, commanded that he be redeemed, as it is written: "The redemption of the first-born, when he is one month old, shall be five shekels, after the sanctuary shekel, or twenty gerahs." An additional verse states: "Sanctify the first-born in Israel, both man and beast, they are Mine."

khor hazeh, sh'hegia z'man pidyono.

I am the messenger of the father of this first-born child, whose time has arrived to be redeemed.[21]

The Cohen asks the emissary:

מַאי בָּעִית טְפֵי, אַתָּה הַשָּׁלִיחַ בְּשֵׁם שׁוֹלְחָךָ, לִתֵּן לִי בֶּן הַבְּכוֹר שֶׁהוּא פֶּטֶר רֶחֶם לְאִמּוֹ, אוֹ בָּעִית לִפְדוֹתוֹ בִּשְׁלִיחוּת אֲבִי הַבְּכוֹר בְּעַד חָמֵשׁ סְלָעִים כִּדְמְחוּיָיב מִדְּאוֹרַיְיתָא?

Mai ba'ith t'fai, ata hashaliach b'shaim sholchakha, litain li ben hab'khor shehu peter rechem l'imo, o ba'ith lifdotho bishlichuth avi hab'khor b'ad chamaish sela'im k'd'm'chuyav mid'Oraytha?

You are a messenger, and you represent the man who sent you. Do you prefer to give me this child or would you rather redeem him as an agent of his father for five *sela'im* which are required by the Torah?

The emissary responds to the question, gives the Cohen the five shekels, and then offers two blessings:

חָפֵץ אֲנִי לִפְדוֹת אֶת הַבְּכוֹר בִּשְׁלִיחוּת אֲבִי הַבְּכוֹר הַזֶּה וְהֵילָךְ דְּמֵי פִּדְיוֹנוֹ מִן הַשּׁוֹלֵחַ, כִּדְמְחוּיָיב מִדְּאוֹרַיְיתָא.

Chafaitz ani lif'doth eth hab'khor bishlichut avi hab'khor hazeh, v'hailakh d'mai fid'yono min hasholaiach k'di'm'chuyav mid'O'rai'tha.

I want to redeem the first-born, in accordance with the wishes of his father, and take this redemption which he gave me to fulfill the requirement of the Torah.

בָּרוּךְ אַתָּה יְיָ אֱלֹהֵינוּ מֶלֶךְ הָעוֹלָם, אֲשֶׁר קִדְּשָׁנוּ בְּמִצְוֹתָיו וְצִוָּנוּ עַל פִּדְיוֹן הַבֵּן.

בָּרוּךְ אַתָּה יְיָ אֱלֹהֵינוּ מֶלֶךְ הָעוֹלָם, שֶׁהֶחֱיָנוּ וְקִיְּמָנוּ וְהִגִּיעָנוּ, לַזְּמַן הַזֶּה:

Barukh ata Adonoy, Elohainu Melekh ha'olam asher kid'shanu b'Mitz'vo'thav v'tzivanu al pidyon haben.

Blessed are You, Lord our God, King of the universe, who sanctified us with Your commandments and commanded us concerning the redemption of the first-born.[22]

Barukh ata Adonoy, Elohainu Melekh ha'olam she'he'che'yanu v'kimanu v'higiyanu lazman hazeh.

Blessed are You, Lord our God, King of the universe, who kept us alive, sustained us, and enabled us to reach this season.[23]

The Cohen holds the redemption over the child's head and says:

זֶה תַּחַת זֶה, זֶה חִלּוּף זֶה, זֶה מָחוּל עַל זֶה; וְיִכָּנֵס זֶה הַבֵּן לְחַיִּים, לְתוֹרָה וּלְיִרְאַת שָׁמָיִם. יְהִי רָצוֹן, שֶׁכְּשֵׁם שֶׁנִּכְנַס לַפִּדְיוֹן, כֵּן יִכָּנֵס לְתוֹרָה וּלְחֻפָּה וּלְמַעֲשִׂים טוֹבִים, אָמֵן.

Zeh tachath zeh, zeh chiluf zeh, zeh machul al zeh. V'yikanais zeh haben l'chayim, l'Thorah ul'yirath shamayim. Y'hi ratzon, she'k'shaim shenikhnas lapid'yon kain yikanais l'Thorah, ul'chupah, ul'ma'asim tovim. Amen.

This is instead of that; this in exchange for that; this is in remission of that. May this child enter into a life of Torah and Godliness. Even as he has been admitted to redemption, so may he enter into Torah, the wedding canopy, and to a life of good deeds. Amen.[24]

The Cohen places his hand on the head of the child and blesses him:

יְשִׂימְךָ אֱלֹהִים כְּאֶפְרַיִם וְכִמְנַשֶּׁה. יְבָרֶכְךָ יְיָ וְיִשְׁמְרֶךָ. יָאֵר יְיָ פָּנָיו אֵלֶיךָ וִיחֻנֶּךָּ. יִשָּׂא יְיָ פָּנָיו אֵלֶיךָ, וְיָשֵׂם לְךָ שָׁלוֹם. יְיָ שׁוֹמְרֶךָ, יְיָ צִלְּךָ עַל יַד יְמִינֶךָ. כִּי אֹרֶךְ יָמִים וּשְׁנוֹת חַיִּים וְשָׁלוֹם יוֹסִיפוּ לָךְ. יְיָ יִשְׁמָרְךָ מִכָּל רָע, יִשְׁמוֹר אֶת נַפְשֶׁךָ. אָמֵן.

God make you like Ephraim and Manasseh.[25] The Lord bless you and sustain you; the Lord cause His face to shine on you and be gracious to you; the Lord grant you peace.[26]

The Lord will protect you from all evil; He will always be near you.[27] May you be blessed with a long and happy life. The Lord will guard you from all evil, He will protect your life.[28]

The Cohen lifts the goblet and offers the blessing for wine:

בָּרוּךְ אַתָּה יְיָ אֱלֹהֵינוּ מֶלֶךְ הָעוֹלָם, בּוֹרֵא פְּרִי הַגָּפֶן.

Blessed are You, Lord our God, King of the universe, who creates the fruit of the vine.

The assembled may now enjoy the repast which is a festive meal (Seudath Mitzvah). At the conclusion Grace After Meals is said (see Chapter 11).

REDEMPTION WITHOUT THE INFANT AT THE CEREMONY

Another option is possible if the father is away when the infant reaches thirty-one days of age. He may obtain the services of a *Cohen* and have the redemption without the child being physically present at the ceremony. Once again the declaration of the father and his dialogue with the *Cohen* must be in accordance with the circumstances.

The father says:

יֵשׁ לִי בֵּן בְּכוֹר וְהוּא פֶּטֶר רֶחֶם לְאִמּוֹ, וְהַקָּדוֹשׁ בָּרוּךְ הוּא צִוָּה הוּא לִפְדּוֹתוֹ, שֶׁנֶּאֱמַר: וּפְדוּיָו מִבֶּן חֹדֶשׁ תִּפְדֶּה בְּעֶרְכְּךָ כֶּסֶף חֲמֵשֶׁת שְׁקָלִים, בְּשֶׁקֶל הַקֹּדֶשׁ, עֶשְׂרִים גֵּרָה הוּא. וְנֶאֱמַר: קַדֶּשׁ־לִי כָל בְּכוֹר; פֶּטֶר כָּל רֶחֶם בִּבְנֵי יִשְׂרָאֵל, בָּאָדָם וּבַבְּהֵמָה, לִי הוּא.

Yaish li ben b'khor v'hu peter rechem l'imo, v'Hakadosh barukh Hu tziva lifdotho, she'-ne'e'mar: "Ufduyav miben chodesh tifdeh b'er'k'kha kesef chamaisheth sh'kalim, b'shekel hakodesh, esrim gerah hu." V'ne'e'mar: "Kadaish Li khal b'khor, peter kal rechem bivnai Yisrael, ba'adam u'vabhaima Li hu."

I am blessed with a child who is his mother's first-born. And the Holy One, blessed be He, commanded that he be redeemed, as it is written: "The redemption of the first-born, when he is one month old, shall be five shekels, after the sanctuary shekel, or twenty gerahs." An additional verse states: "Sanctify the first-born, the first-born in Israel, both man and beast, they are Mine."[29]

The Cohen asks the father:

מַאי בָּעִית טְפֵי לִתֵּן לִי, בִּנְךָ בְּכוֹרְךָ שֶׁהוּא פֶּטֶר רֶחֶם לְאִמּוֹ, אוֹ בָּעִית לִפְדוֹתוֹ בְּעַד חָמֵשׁ סְלָעִים, כִּדְמְחַיַּבְתְּ מִדְּאוֹרַיְתָא?

Mai ba'ith t'fai litain li, binkha b'khorkha shehu peter rechem l'imo, o ba'ith lifdotho b'ad chamaish sela'im kid'm'chuyavt mid'Oraytha?

Do you prefer to give me your son, or would you rather redeem him for five *sela'im*, which you are required to give according to the Torah?[30]

The father responds to the question, gives the Cohen the five shekels, and then offers two blessings:

חָפֵץ אֲנִי לִפְדוֹת אֶת בְּנִי, וְהֵילָךְ דְּמֵי פִדְיוֹנוֹ, כִּדְמְחַיַּבְתִּי מִדְּאוֹרַיְתָא. בָּרוּךְ אַתָּה יְיָ אֱלֹהֵינוּ מֶלֶךְ הָעוֹלָם, אֲשֶׁר קִדְּשָׁנוּ בְּמִצְוֹתָיו וְצִוָּנוּ עַל פִּדְיוֹן הַבֵּן.

בָּרוּךְ אַתָּה יְיָ אֱלֹהֵינוּ מֶלֶךְ הָעוֹלָם, שֶׁהֶחֱיָנוּ וְקִיְּמָנוּ וְהִגִּיעָנוּ, לַזְּמַן הַזֶּה.

Chafaitz ani lif'doth eth b'ni,

I want to redeem my son, and

v'hailakh d'mai fid'yono, k'di'm'chu'yavti mid'Orai'tha.

take the redemption, which I am required to give according to the Torah.[31]

Barukh ata Adonoy, Elohainu Melekh ha'olam asher kid'-shanu b'mitz'vo'thav v'tzivanu al pidyon haben.

Blessed are You, Lord our God, King of the universe, who sanctified us with Your commandments and commanded us concerning the redemption of the first-born.[32]

Barukh ata Adonoy, Elohainu Melekh ha'olam she'he'che'ya-nu v'kimanu v'higiyanu laz-man hazeh.

Blessed are You, Lord our God, King of the universe, who kept us alive, sustained us, and enabled us to reach this season.[33]

The Cohen continues:

זֶה תַּחַת בִּנְךָ, זֶה חִילוּף בִּנְךָ, זֶה מָחוּל עַל בִּנְךָ. יָצָא זֶה לַכֹּהֵן וְיִכָּנֵס לְחַיִּים, לְתוֹרָה, וּלְיִרְאַת שָׁמָיִם. יְהִי רָצוֹן שֶׁכְּשֵׁם שֶׁנִּכְנַס לַפִּדְיוֹן, כֵּן יִכָּנֵס לְתוֹרָה, וּלְחֻפָּה, וּלְמַעֲשִׂים טוֹבִים. וְנֹאמַר אָמֵן.

Zeh tachath binkha, zeh chiluf binkha, zeh machul al binkha. Yatza zeh laCohen v'yikanais l'chayim, l'Thorah ul'yirath shamayim. Y'hi ratzon sh'k'shaim sh'nikhnas lapid-yon, kain y'kanais l'Thorah, ul'chupa, ul'ma'asim tovim. V'nomar Amen.

This is instead of your son; this is in exchange for your son; this is in remission of your son. May your son enter into a life of Torah and Godliness. Even as he has been admitted to redemption, so may he enter into Torah, the wedding canopy, and to a life of good deeds. And let us say, Amen.[34]

The Cohen lifts the goblet and offers the blessing for wine:

בָּרוּךְ אַתָּה יְיָ אֱלֹהֵינוּ מֶלֶךְ הָעוֹלָם, בּוֹרֵא פְּרִי הַגָּפֶן.

Blessed are You, Lord our God, King of the universe, who creates the fruit of the vine.

THE SEPHARDIC RITE

The Sephardic rite contains all the elements that appear in the Ashkenazic rite, but it omits the father's declaration and the dialogue between the father and the *Cohen*. The *Cohen* ascertains that the child is the mother's first-born and then proceeds with the rite.[35]

The Cohen says:

זֶה הַבֵּן בְּכוֹר הוּא. וְהַקָּדוֹשׁ בָּרוּךְ הוּא צִוָּה לִפְדּוֹתוֹ. שֶׁנֶּאֱמַר: וּפְדוּיָו מִבֶּן
חֹדֶשׁ תִּפְדֶּה. בְּעֶרְכְּךָ כֶּסֶף חֲמֵשֶׁת שְׁקָלִים בְּשֶׁקֶל הַקֹּדֶשׁ. עֶשְׂרִים גֵּרָה
הוּא: כְּשֶׁהָיִיתָ בִּמְעֵי אִמֶּךָ. הָיִיתָ בִּרְשׁוּת אָבִיךָ שֶׁבַּשָּׁמַיִם. וּבִרְשׁוּת אָבִיךָ
וְאִמֶּךָ: עַכְשָׁיו אַתָּה בִּרְשׁוּתִי שֶׁאֲנִי כֹהֵן. וְאָבִיךָ וְאִמֶּךָ מְבַקְשִׁים לִפְדּוֹתְךָ.
שֶׁאַתָּה בְּכוֹר מְקֻדָּשׁ. שֶׁכֵּן כָּתוּב. וַיְדַבֵּר יְיָ אֶל־מֹשֶׁה לֵּאמֹר: קַדֶּשׁ־לִי כָל־
בְּכוֹר. פֶּטֶר כָּל־רֶחֶם בִּבְנֵי יִשְׂרָאֵל בָּאָדָם וּבַבְּהֵמָה לִי הוּא.

Zeh haben b'khor hu, v'Hakadosh barukh Hu tziva lifdotho, she'ne'e'mar: "Ufduyav miben chodesh tifdeh b'er'kha kesef chamaisheth sh'kalim b'shekel hakodesh, esrim gerah hu." K'she'hayita bim'ai im'kha hayita bir'shuth Avikha she'ba'sha'mayim, u'virshuth avikha v'imekha. Akh'shav ata virshuti she'ani khohain. V'avikha v'imekha m'vakshim lif'dothekha sheata b'khor m'kudash. Sh'kain katuv: "Vai'dabair Adonoy el Moshe laimor: 'kadaish Li khol b'khor peter kol rechem bivnai Yisrael, ba'adam u'vab'haima Li hu.'"

This child is a first-born son, and the Holy One, blessed be He, commanded that he be redeemed, as it is written: "The redemption of the first-born, when he is one month old, shall be five shekels, after the sanctuary shekel, or twenty gerahs." When you were in your mother's body, you belonged to God and to your father and mother. Now you belong to me, since I am a *Cohen*. Your father and mother are requesting that you be redeemed from your sanctity of being a sacred first-born. It is written in the Torah: "God spoke to Moses, saying, 'Sanctify the first-born in Israel, both man and beast, they are Mine.'"[36]

The father offers two blessings:

בָּרוּךְ אַתָּה יְיָ אֱלֹהֵינוּ מֶלֶךְ הָעוֹלָם אֲשֶׁר קִדְּשָׁנוּ בְּמִצְוֹתָיו וְצִוָּנוּ עַל פִּדְיוֹן הַבֵּן.

בָּרוּךְ אַתָּה יְיָ אֱלֹהֵינוּ מֶלֶךְ הָעוֹלָם שֶׁהֶחֱיָנוּ וְקִיְּמָנוּ וְהִגִּיעָנוּ לַזְּמַן הַזֶּה.

Barukh ata Adonoy, Elohainu Melekh ha'olam, asher kid'shanu b'mitz'vo'thav v'tzivanu al pidyon haben.

Blessed are You, Lord our God, King of the universe, who sanctified us with Your commandments and commanded us concerning the redemption of the first-born.[37]

Barukh ata Adonoy, Elohainu Melekh ha'olam, she'he'che'yanu v'kimanu v'higiyanu lazman hazeh.

Blessed are You, Lord our God, King of the universe, who kept us alive, sustained us, and enabled us to reach this season.[38]

The father gives the Cohen five shekels and the Cohen blesses the child:

קִבַּלְתִּי מִמְּךָ חֲמֵשׁ סְלָעִים אֵלּוּ בְּפִדְיוֹן בִּנְךָ זֶה. וַהֲרֵי הוּא פָּדוּי בָּהֶן. כְּדַת מֹשֶׁה וְיִשְׂרָאֵל: יְהִי רָצוֹן מִלִּפְנֵי אֱלֹהֵינוּ שֶׁבַּשָּׁמַיִם. כְּמוֹ שֶׁזָּכִיתָ לְפִדְיוֹן הַבֵּן. כַּךְ תִּזְכֶּה לְקַיֵּם כָּל־הַמִּצְוֹת שֶׁבַּתּוֹרָה.

Kibalti mim'kha chamaish selaim ailu b'fidyon binkha zeh. V'harai hu faduy bahain k'dath Moshe v'Yisrael. Y'hi ratzon milif'nai Elohainu she'ba'sha'ma'yim k'mo shezakhitha l'fidyon haben kakh tizkeh l'kayaim kal hamitzvoth shebaTorah.

I received from you five shekels as the redemption of your son. He is redeemed in accordance with the law of Moses and Israel. May it be the will of our God in heaven that just as you have been privileged to redeem your son, so may you be privileged to fulfill all the *mitzvoth* in the Torah.[39]

APPENDIX 1
Anatomy of the Penis

The first section of this appendix outlines the gross anatomy of the penis. The second is a discussion of the prepuce and related structures.[1] The latter material is most germane to *Brith Milah*. In the interest of simplicity, a brief description will serve as a review for those familiar with the anatomy and as a general overview for individuals reading the material for the first time.

THE PENIS

The body of the penis is comprised of three elongated masses of tissue which become enlarged when they are engorged with blood during erection. These include two *corpora cavernosa* and one *corpus spongiosum*. The latter lies in a groove of the conjoined cavernosa. These three *cavernosa* are fixed to the pubic bone. The urethra is situated in the *corpus spongiosum* and terminates at the *meatus*, the opening for voiding urine. It was noted earlier that there can be anomalies where the meatus is not located precisely at the tip.[2]

Distally (externally, at the periphery of the penis), the *corpus spongiosum* expands in a conical shape, similar in appearance to an acorn. This enlargement is called the *glans* (Latin for "acorn"). The base of the glans has a projecting rim, the *corona*, or crown, and it overhangs a constriction, the neck of the penis. Both the corona and the neck of the penis have small glands which secrete *smegma*, a soft creamy material.

THE PREPUCE

The skin covering the penis is very thin and elastic, enabling it to expand during an erection. This skin covers the entire penis, the shaft as well as the corona. At the neck it seperates from the glans and merely hangs over it. At the point of separation, the skin doubles back toward the corona. This is the *prepuce*. It is the extension of the original skin covering the penile shaft.

Immediately under the prepuce is the *mucous membrane,* a white, glistening structure. This is the lining of the urethra; it continues past the external urethral meatus and covers the glans. At the corona it unites with the prepuce.

The skin of the penis is a continuation of the skin of the abdomen on the dorsal, or upper side, and of the scrotum on the ventral, or under side. The *mohel* must be very careful to avoid including the skin of the scrotum when he excises the prepuce, and he must be especially cautious not to enter the meatus when he separates the mucous membrane from the glans.

The arteries and the veins of the penis are submerged within the organ. Consequently, no blood vessel is likely to be cut during the circumcision of the infant. In the event that a small vein is severed, the bleeding may be readily controlled by exerting pressure with a finger and then applying a pressure bandage. Cutting the *frenulum,* however, will result in hemorrhage because it is endowed with a good supply of blood.

APPENDIX 2
Technique

ASEPSIS

The primary concern of the *mohel* when circumcising is to avoid harming the baby. There is always a possibility that micro-organisms will gain entrance to the wound. To prevent this, the *mohel* washes his hands with Betadine, a disinfectant used in most nurseries. There are no bacteria resistant to it when it is used for at least five minutes. When the *mohel* washes his hands in Betadine or a Betadine-like agent for fifteen minutes, he can be assured that he has eliminated all the bacteria that may be contaminating his hands.

Physicians do not insist that the *mohel* wear surgical gloves or a mask. However, when a *mohel* comes in contact with infants from a nursery with a serious Staphylococcus or a pathogenic enteric organism, he should routinely use gloves to eliminate the possibility of hand colonization.[1]

The *mohel's* instruments are sterilized before he comes to the *brith*. There are several ways that sterilization can be effected: (1) boiling the instruments in water for ten minutes; (2) exposing the instruments to 70 percent alcohol for one hour; (3) autoclaving; or (4) using a gas ampule which is employed by ophthalmologists.[2] The dressings, too, must be sterile. They can be purchased to conform to the needed sizes.

Betadine should be thoroughly applied to the areas of circumcision; merely swabbing it on is not sufficient. The *mohel* must allow time for the Betadine to be effective.

Parents should be assured that because this is a well-vascularized, open area, the risk of infection is minimal.

127

It is recommended that the people in attendance remain at a distance from the *mohel* as he performs the rite. Peering over his shoulder makes his effort difficult. The only people who should be near the *mohel* and the baby are the infant's father and the *sandek*.

PROCEDURE

This guide is not meant to be a training manual. In this section I will simply list and explain briefly the steps needed to accomplish the holy task. A beginner should not assume that it contains sufficient information to allow him to perform a *brith*. He needs the help of the preceptor to avoid pitfalls.

The *sandek* is seated on a chair with his feet elevated several inches on a stool. He keeps his legs closely together. A pillow is placed on his lap, and the infant is put on the pillow facing the *mohel*. When the necessary clothing has been removed from the child, his thighs and knees are bent up. The thighs are then rotated outward, and are kept firmly in place by the *sandek* until the conclusion of the *Brith Milah*.

In *Brith Milah* the *mohel* removes the skin which covers the whole of the glans before an erection is effected. The mucous membrane, which is situated immediately underneath the prepuce, need not be excised. It is sufficient to tear it. There are two basic ways to accomplish these objectives. The first consists of two separate actions: (a) cutting off the prepuce, and (b) tearing the membrane up the center.

The second method is to excise the prepuce and the mucous membrane simultaneously. This is the approach taken by most *mohelim* and is approved by the majority of rabbinic authorities.[3] Circumcision by the second method requires that a probe, a blunt thin metal rod, be inserted under the mucous membrane and swept around the glans to break any existing adhesion.[4] The mucous membrane may be very tightly attached to the glans or only loosely attached. Extreme care must be taken not to enter the meatus.

The *mohel* holds the prepuce and the mucous membrane firmly with his thumb, index finger, and middle finger. He measures off the amount to be excised with his eyes and the sensitivity of his fingers. He takes the shield with his free hand and places the prepuce and the mucous membrane held by his fingers into the slit of the shield at precisely the level of his fingers.

The shield is a flat piece of metal with a center slit. Its edges are made to grasp at the level to be cut. The *mohel* generally carries various slit sizes. The shield pulls the prepuce and the mucous membrane forward and protects the glans penis and the scrotum.

The shield, held in the hand, must be inclined towards the abdomen of the child. The cut is made at a slant since the upper part of the penis (the 12 o'clock portion) extends further than the 6 o'clock part.[5] The *mohel* must be careful that the skin of the scrotum is not caught in the shield.

When the probe is not used to clear the adhesions, another step, *p'riah* ("uncovering"), is required. After the prepuce is removed, there is an opening in the mucous membrane. The *mohel* inserts the nail of his thumb and takes hold of the membrane. Then he achieves a similar hold with his other thumbnail. The *mohel* tears the mucous membrane straight up to the corona and rolls both sides back. He must know how much pressure to exert. These two sections of the mucous membrane serve as the beginning of the bandaging, which will be discussed below.

The next stage, *metzitzah,* involves the direct suction of the wound by mouth. The sources of the practice of *metzitzah* indicate that it was necessary to protect the health of the baby. Consequently, failing to carry out this measure was regarded as a serious risk to the infant.[6]

Since the time of Rabbi Moshe (Schreiber) Sofer (1762–1839), author of the *Chatham Sofer,* there has been a protracted debate among rabbinic authorities. Rabbi Sofer pointed out that the Mishnah does not specify how the drawing of the blood "from the distant places" is to be done. Since there is danger of infection from direct suction of the mouth, *metzitzah* is generally performed with the barrel of a syringe, containing a piece of absorbent cotton.[7] The rounded end of the tube is placed over the penis and pressed firmly on the area of the lower abdomen surrounding the root of the penis. Suction by mouth is carried out through the flattened end of the tube. Another method involves pressing gauze on the wound so that the blood will be drawn out.

Mohelim who have direct mouth contact with the wound first rinse their mouths carefully with alcohol. This precaution, however, is not sufficient to make the oral cavity sterile. Direct mouth contact should, therefore, be avoided, and one of the aforementioned methods substituted.[8] When utilizing the thumbnails for *p'riah,* special precautions must be taken.

The concluding stage is to bandage the penis with a dry bandage which is covered with a Vaselinated bandage. The bandage must be slightly loose, to allow some blood to exude in order that a clot may set in. If the bandages are too tight, no blood will flow out. Thus there will be no clotting, and when the bandages are removed the bleeding will start again. Furthermore, a very tight bandage will constrict the penis and prevent the baby from urinating properly. *Mohelim* have practiced the art of proper bandage application over a period of 3,700 years, long before the suture was developed.

The next change that took place in circumcision technique was the introduction of the Gomco Clamp by physicians. The Union of Orthodox Rabbis ruled against the use of this clamp.[9] *Mohelim* were in a quandary. They would not ignore the ruling of the rabbis, but the instrument was helpful in preventing postcircumcision bleeding. Furthermore, numerous hospitals required its use when *Brith Milah* took place in their facilities.

Hoping to overcome the strictures of the rabbinic organization, a *mohel* invented the Magen Clamp.[10]

The debate continues unabated. Consequently, no definitive decision can be rendered.

HEALING TIME

Parents are often concerned with the amount of time that it

will take for the circumcision to heal. There is no fixed answer because infants, like adults, heal at different rates. Once the complete healing has taken place, the parents will have a good idea of how rapid or slow a healer their baby will be.

APPENDIX 3
Circumcision—Pro and Con

The overwhelming majority of boys in the United States—both Jewish and non-Jewish—are circumcised. It is estimated that 1.5 million boys are circumcised annually in this country. Most physicians advise non-Jewish parents to have their sons circumcised because they feel that it promotes better hygiene. There are, however, some doctors who maintain that circumcision is unnecessary. Negative opinions have been published in medical journals, and these views have received wide circulation in the media from coast to coast.

It should be pointed out that there are two reasons for performing a circumcision. The first is ritual, or *Brith Milah*. The second is routine and is performed by physicians, solely for health reasons, on non-Jewish boys. Most physicians who feel that circumcision is medically unnecessary respect *Brith Milah,* and they state unequivocally that their opposition is only to routine circumcision. Unfortunately, there are physicians and laymen who use this controversy as an opportunity to attack the practice of *Brith Milah.*

The Jewish community must recognize that in time the constant attacks on routine circumcision may erode our people's loyalty even to *Brith Milah.* The false statements that are made in reputable periodicals may influence Jewish parents to the extent that they will deny their sons the right to be brought into the Covenant of Abraham. We dare not be silent, therefore, in the face of such persistent attacks.

Articles on circumcision have appeared in medical journals,[1] newspapers,[2] popular magazines,[3] and scholarly periodicals.[4] Books have been written on each side of the controversy.[5] Television, too, has joined in the fray.[6]

On January 24, 1979, the *New York Times* printed an article by

Jane E. Brody which restated the arguments. The *Jewish Week* asked Dr. Elliot Leiter to respond to the *Times* article.[7] Dr. Leiter is director of Urology at the Beth Israel Medical Center and professor and acting chairman of the Department of Urology at the Mount Sinai School of Medicine of the City University of New York. His response is presented in its entirety because of its importance. Dr. Leiter wrote:

> In her recent article on the pros and cons of circumcision, Jane Brody is guilty of the most subtle and dangerous kind of propaganda. Under the guise of presenting an objective assessment of the benefits and risks of circumcision, she has misrepresented facts, omitted pertinent data, distorted statistics and promulgated obvious inconsistencies. The final result is anything but a dispassionate discussion of the pros and cons of circumcision.
>
> As a practicing pediatric urologist and as an affiliate fellow of The American Academy of Pediatrics, I fully subscribe to the findings of the Ad Hoc Committee of the Academy that there are "no absolute medical indications for routine circumcision of the new born."[8] Many parents, however, usually for religious reasons, are anxious to have a circumcision during the first week of life.[9] For these parents, it is imperative that the record be set straight regarding the statistically substantiable data in this highly charged and overly emotional area, where diatribe has often replaced reason. Prejudicial presentations, such as those of Ms. Brody, cannot be left to stand as a final statement.
>
> First, the mis-statement of fact and the distortion of statistics.
> Jane Brody: " . . . Among men who have poor hygiene, circumcision offers little protection (against penile cancer)."
> Dr. Leiter: All studies have stressed that, in poor countries where soap is expensive and water relatively unavailable, penile cancer is up to 10 times more common than in those countries with high standards of personal care. Even within one country, differences felt to be entirely attributable to standards of cleanliness have been demonstrated. For example, in the United States, it has been estimated that penile cancer is two to four times more common in blacks than in whites.
> The evidence that circumcision dramatically reduces the inci-

dence of cancer of the penis is virtually irrefutable. For example, in Uganda, where circumcision is rarely performed, penile cancers are more than six times as common in Kenya where the majority of Africans are circumcised. Even in Uganda, only one case of penile cancer (out of a total of 508 cases) was reported in the Gisu tribe, the only tribe in Uganda to practice circumcision. Conversely, the Luo tribe of Kenya, which does not practice circumcision, showed an incidence of penile cancer of 14.5%! Similarly, in India, the difference in incidence between the Hindu and Moslem populations is quite striking. Only 25 of 1,336 cases of penile cancer reported by Wolbarst occurred in Moslems who ordinarily undergo circumcision between the ages of four and nine years. Not only does circumcision reduce the incidence of penile cancer but circumcision at birth virtually provides lifelong immunity to this disease.

Jane Brody: "Penile cancer is rare, in any case, and usually not fatal."

Dr. Leiter: While it is true that in the United States, cancer of the penis constitutes only 1-2% of cancers in males, in the Far East, Africa and in the West Indies, it makes up more than 10% of male cancers. If discovered early, the cure rate, with the most modern and sophisticated methods, ranges from 50-90%. Although radiation has been successfully used in very small lesions, treatment generally requires at least partial amputation of the penis and often involves much more extensive and disfiguring surgery. If unsuccessfully treated 90% of patients will die of their disease within five years, generally of local recurrence in groin and penis with local ulceration, hemorrhage and infection.

Jane Brody: "More babies suffer major complications from circumcision (2 per 1,000). . . . serious mishaps . . . include the development of a widespread and potentially fatal infection, excessive loss of penile skin necessitating grafting, and gangrene and sloughing off of the penis."

Dr. Leiter: In a study of 1964, of those children circumcised ritually by experienced *mohelim* in Jerusalem, one child in 800 had to be admitted to the hospital, because of excessive bleeding which was easily controlled. In fact, J.P. Blandy, Professor of Urology at the University of London, has observed as follows: "The Jewish rite deserves careful study by any doctor called upon to circumcise a baby. No surgeon could fail to profit from a study of the handbook drawn up for the instruction of *mohelim,* which is a model of good sense and sound surgical principles, and if the surgeon really wants to know how skillfully the operation can be done, he should solicit the privilege of being present at one of these ceremonies. He will witness a technique that bears comparison with that of any master surgeon." I might add that a similar standard has been set for more than a decade by the Brith Milah Board of New York of the New York Board of Rabbis.

Additionally, while cataloguing the horrors associated with circumcision, the most commonly occurring sequeleum—namely, urethral meatal stenosis—was barely mentioned by Miss Brody. This narrowing of the opening of the urinary tract at the tip of the penis is generally preventable by frequent diaper changes in the first six to eight months of life; a fact which parents contemplating circumcision of their infant have a right to know, and which Miss Brody had an obligation to present.

Major internal inconsistencies in the article attest to the lack of attention to detail which is evident throughout Brody's presentation. In at least one instance, this results in presentation of a course of management that is, to say the least, less than optimal. For example, the following; "Some 96% of newborn boys are born with phimosis, but the vast majority will outgrow it."

This is incontestably true. But why then, the suggestion that "the pediatrician break the natural adhesions of the foreskin to the penis when the infant is about three to four weeks of age . . ."? In 90% of little boys, these adhesions will spontaneously disappear, *if they are left undisturbed.* Premature lysis is not only unnecessary but will predispose to the development of further adhesions that greatly increase the likelihood that subsequent circumcision will be necessary.

As another example, Brody suggests that "circumcision of the newborn . . . cannot be said to be painless or free of psycholgical trauma," but goes on to state that psychological trauma from the surgery is least likely to occur if done before the child starts school! Such a statement hardly deserves further comment! When expertly performed by an experienced *mohel,* newborn circumcision, without the need for anaesthesia, is over in less than a minute. At age 3 or 4 years, circumcision requires general anesthesia and, as observed by Professor Blandy, "is time-consuming and delicate."

Lastly, while, as stated "good penile hygiene is an adequate alternative to circumcision," Miss Brody fails to appreciate that for those of us who examine the male genitalia day in and day out, it is obvious that this goal is not so easily attainable as she may think. In this context, the gratuitous statement by Dr. Grimes that "surgery is not recommended to foster cleanliness of the ears, fingernails and vulva of women" (in contrast to the ears and fingernails of men, I presume) is especially annoying. Aside from the obvious fact that cancer of the fingernails has never been reported—either in males or females—because they were dirty, I might also offer in refutation a comment by Dr. Joseph Kaufman, presently Professor of Urology at the University of California in Los Angeles, who stated that "as a urologist who sees boys and men at all ages, I can say that the circumcised penis is clean and the uncircumcised one all too often is not." Until such time as the major soap manufacturers add a penile hygiene preparation to their vaginal douches, toothpastes and deodorants, I'm afraid we will have to accept human nature as it is.

In view of the foregoing, the following conclusions should be presented to all parents before they consent to circumcision of their infant:

1. There are no absolute medical indications for routine circumcision of the newborn.[10] Certainly, circumcision should *never* be done on a child who is not absolutely well.

2. Ritual circumcision when performed expertly by a trained *mohel* has a complication rate of less than 0.13%. Most of these complications consist of excessive bleeding which can be corrected without permanent sequelae.

3. Circumcision at birth virtually prevents the later development of penile cancer. It affords this prophylaxis by facilitating personal hygiene. While optimal hygiene apparently gives the same protection, practically speaking, such standards of cleanliness are not always attainable. In any case, they will be impossible in the 5–10% in whom the normal phimotic adhesions do not spontaneously disappear. In these children, circumcision at age 3–4 years is necessary. At this age, general anesthesia is required. Except for meatal stenosis, all the complications that occur with newborn circumcision can be expected at this age as well.

4. Narrowing of the meatal opening is much more common after newborn circumcision but can generally be avoided by frequent diaper changes and scrupulous care in the first 6–8 months of life.

5. If a child is not circumcised in the newborn period the adhe-

sions between the glans penis and foreskin will spontaneously disappear in more than 90% of children before the age of three years. They should *not* be broken by the pediatrician at 3–4 weeks of age since this will probably increase the likelihood of eventual circumcision.

We are grateful to Dr. Elliot Leiter for his authoritative opinion.

The television program referred to above was a source of concern to many. The observant Jewish community, on the whole, was unaware of the program since it appeared on a Friday night. A reading of the transcript revealed that the same arguments that had appeared elsewhere were repeated on national television. The argument of the baby having "pain" during the circumcision needs clarification. Dr. Leiter was consulted for his expert opinion. This is his reply:[11]

> There is no doubt that circumcision, without anesthesia is painful, but the use of language such as "circumcision hurts like crazy" or a clamp "crushes" the blood vessels adds an inflammatory and judgmental tone to what should otherwise be a dispassionate description. The amount of pain is relatively minor, even in adults, where the operation can be done easily under local anesthesia. In general, the glans penis contains many more nerve endings than does the foreskin which is not as sensitive as most people would think. Consequently, even in the post-operation period, most adult patients will need little more for pain medication than a couple of Tylenols every few hours for the first few days. Additionally, the matter of appreciation of pain in infants is quite a difficult thing to assess. While there is no doubt that they possess nerve endings and that there are local reflex arcs which will result in withdrawal when an extremity is stimulated, pain is, after all, a conscious appreciation of such a local noxious stimulus and no one has yet been able to prove that this conscious appreciation exists in the infant. In fact, developmentally at least, there is evidence to suggest that the spinal pathways from the extremities to the cerebral area mature only slowly and gradually and are far from fully developed in early infancy.

Dr. Leiter also provided these comments on the "NBC Magazine" television program:

Dr. [William] Gole states that "Circumcision does not prevent penile cancer in males." You, of course, know that this is absolutely not the case. While it is true that good personal hygiene can accomplish virtually the same effect, this can be accomplished only in the freely retractable foreskin. In general, approximately 10% of all males will eventually be unable to fully retract their foreskin and for these men circumcision would provide life-long immunity to the development of penile cancer.

Dr. [Paul] Fleiss takes the Academy of Pediatrics statement well beyond the bounds of rationality when he states there are "no valid medical reasons for doing a circumcision today." First, there is no doubt in anyone's mind that there are certainly very valid medical reasons for doing circumcisions in adults and no one would argue the fact that there are certainly medical reasons for doing circumcisions on some children, as well.

Dr. [Jay] Gordon states that there is a significant risk to circumcision and states that there is a "serious medical complication in one out of every five-hundred circumcisions." He never characterizes what these "serious" medical complications are, but most studies fail to show anything more serious than quite minor complications, such as somewhat prolonged bleeding that is easily controlled.

Dr. [David] Grimes never states how he arrives at his estimate of the cost of circumcision, nor does he estimate what the costs of hospitalization for balanitis, balano-posthitis and cancer of the penis are. All of these diseases can be prevented by circumcision. In order to know whether circumcision is cost-effective or not, one should compare the cost of circumcision to the cost of treating the diseases which would be prevented by doing circumcision.

The only discussant with whom I can agree fully is Dr. [John] Duckett. I would note his closing statement, namely that "the subject is so overladen with these overtones of social, cultural, sexual and religious factors that have obviously colored the opinions of all the people that have taken a firm anti-circumcision stand in this NBC piece."

A more rational and dispassionate view could be summarized as follows:

While there are no absolute medical indications for routine circumcision of the newborn, ritual circumcision when performed expertly by a trained *mohel* has a minor complication rate of less than 0.13%. Most of these complications consist of excessive bleeding, which can be corrected without permanent sequelae.

Circumcision at birth virtually prevents the latter development of penile cancer. It affords this prophylaxis by facilitating personal hygiene. While optimal hygiene apparently gives the same protection, practically speaking such standards of cleanliness are not always attainable. In any case, it would be impossible in the five to ten percent of males in whom the normal phimotic adhesions do not spontaneously disappear. In these children, a circumcision at age 3 to 4 years is necessary. At this age, general anesthesia is required. Except for meatal stenosis, *all* of the complications that occur with newborn circumcision can be expected at this age as well.

Thank you, Dr. Leiter, for providing the facts. The Brith Milah Board does not advocate routine circumcision of the newborn. This is a subject for the parents of the child and their pediatrician. We are certain of the safety, efficacy, and reliability of ritual circumcision, which is the cornerstone of the Jewish religion.

Notes

CHAPTER 1

1. In this volume, *Brith Milah* is also referred to as ritual circumcision, *brith, milah,* and Covenant of Abraham.

2. Genesis 17:7.

3. *Tur, Yoreh Deah* 260.

4. *Menachoth* 43b.

5. *Yevamoth* 72a.

6. I Kings 19:14.

7. The Greeks forbade circumcision. See *Scroll of the Hasmoneans* I:9–10. Rome's decree is found in *Shabbath* 130a and *Rosh Hashanah* 19a. The sacrificial response of our people was an equally determined one.

8. *Otzar Yisrael,* vol. 2, p. 119.

9. Lucy S. Dawidowicz, *The War Against the Jews* (New York: Holt, Rinehart & Winston, 1975).

10. Dov Rosen, *Shema Yisrael,* translated into English by Leonard Oschry from the 4th Hebrew ed. (Israel, Peli Printing), p. 204. The incident was first recorded in *Churban Litah* by Rabbi Ephraim Oshry (New York, 1952).

11. *Nedarim* 32a.

12. *Shabbath* 137b.

13. *Perush HaMishnayoth* on *Shabbath* 19:6 (137a).

14. This quotation is from his lecture delivered at the National Institute of Mental Health Project conducted at Yeshiva University, May 21, 1958.

15. This quotation is from the same series, delivered on February 24, 1959.

16. Rabbi Aryeh Kaplan, *The Handbook of Jewish Thought* (New York: Maznaim, 1979), p. 47.

17. *Kiddushin* 29a, *Yoreh Deah* 260:1.

18. *Yevamoth* 71b; Rashi and Maharsha, loc. cit.; *Or Zarua, Hilkhoth Milah* 96.

19. *Yoreh Deah* 261:1.

20. Rosh on *Chullin* 87a, no. 8.

21. *Hagah, Yoreh Deah* 265:11. When the weather was inclement, the *Brith Milah* took place at home rather than the synagogue.

22. Tosafoth, *Pesachim* 101a, s.v. *D'achli.*

23. *Yalkut Shimoni* on Isaiah, no. 449; Rabbi Yaakov Hagozer, *Zikhron Brith L'Rishonim,* p. 94; Rabbainu Yehudah HaChasid, *Sefer HaChasidim,* p. 1140; Rabbi Isaac Sperling, *Taamai HaMinhagim,* p. 929.

24. Rabbi Yaakov Emden, *Migdal Oz* (Jerusalem: Eshkol, 1974), pp. 288 f.

25. *Yoma* 83b.

26. *Zikhron Brith L'Rishonim* in the *Melu'im* Section cites *Chimudai Doniel* (MS); *Zokher HaBrith* 24:20; *Sepher HaBris*, p. 282; *Assia*, no. 33, pp. 14–21.

CHAPTER 2

1. Genesis 17:11, following Rashi's interpretation.

2. Genesis 17:12.

3. *Shabbath* 132a; *Megillah* 20a; *Yad, Hilkhoth Milah* 1:8; *Hagah, Yoreh Deah* 262:1. Rashba maintains that a circumcision performed prior to the eighth day cannot be validated with the subsequent drawing of a drop of blood, cited by *Hagah, Yoreh Deah* 264:1. See Chapter 9, note 42, to learn why physicians insist that a *brith* should not take place before the eighth day.

4. Mishnah, *Shabbath* 133a. The Hebrew terms will be discussed in Chapter 8.

5. *Yoreh Deah* 266:2.

6. Rabbi Charles B. Chavel's edition of *Kithvai HaRamban, He'Emunah V'Habitachon*, vol. 2, p. 425.

7. *Hagah, Yoreh Deah* 266:14.

8. *Rosh Hashanah* 29b, *Pesachim* 69b, *Sukkah* 42b, *Megillah* 4b.

9. Their comments on *Megillah* 4b.

10. The training of the *mohel* is discussed in Chapter 3.

11. *Shabbath* 134b; *Hagah, Orach Chaim* 331:9.

12. *Orach Chaim* 331:6 forbids having a non-Jew bring the baby from one type of domain to another. However, *Magen Avraham, Orach Chaim* 331:5; *Turai Zahav, Orach Chaim* 349:1; *Hagah, Orach Chaim* 276:2; and *Mishnah B'rurah* 331:6 permit this procedure because many authorities maintain that there is no public domain that meets the halakhic requirements. Consequently a non-Jew may carry the baby for a Jew to the synagogue.

13. Rabbi Moshe Feinstein, *Iggroth Moshe, Yoreh Deah* 156. See article by Rabbi Moshe Pirutinsky in *Hapardes*, Kislev 5732 (1971).

14. *Yad, Milah* 1:18. See *Yoreh Deah* 262:2.

15. Rabbi Moses D. Tendler, in *Symposium on Medical Dilemmas and the Practise of Milah*, p. 35. This is based on *Yoreh Deah* 262:2. The seven-day waiting period commences on the day and the hour when the doctor says that the baby is well.

16. Eugene J. Cohen, Ph.D., and Arthur Eidelman, M.D., *Proceedings of the Symposium on Current Concepts in Pediatrics and Urology and Their Relationship to Brith Milah*, p. 22.

17. *Symposium on Medical Dilemmas and the Practise of Milah,* p. 17.

18. Rabbi Tendler cited a Responsum in *She'eloth Dovid* by Rabbi Dovid Friedman in *Proceedings,* p. 23. A similar view is presented in the *Arukh HaShulchan, Yoreh Deah* 263:4. See article by Dr. Abraham Steinberg in *Assia,* 29/30, (June 1981): 21–42.

CHAPTER 3

1. Genesis 21:4; Mishnah and *B'raitha, Kiddushin* 29a; Mishnah, *Nedarim* 31b; *Yoreh Deah* 260:1.

2. *Sanhedrin* 17b.

3. *Sefer HaZikhronoth,* Maharash Abuhav, *zikhron* 9; *Sefer HaBris,* p. 162, no. 34. Communities that have no Milah Board can achieve the same result when their rabbis and physicians examine the candidate. It is most helpful to the cause of *milah* to form a local Brith Milah Board. The Brith Milah Board of America was established to render every assistance requested by communities in the formation of such a group. Information regarding the creation of a Milah Board can be obtained by contacting the Brith Milah Board of America, 10 East 73rd Street, New York, N.Y. 10021.

4. *Hagah, Yoreh Deah* 264:1.

5. *Zikhron Brith L'Rishonim,* p. 79.

6. Ibid., p. 68.

7. Rashi, *Sanhedrin* 17b, s.v. *Rofeh; Smag,* Positive Commandment 93.

8. *Sefer HaBris,* p. 160, no. 30.

9. There are two views in a case where the circumcision was performed by a *posul.* One opinion is that nothing can correct the damage. See *Avodah Zarah* 26b; *Yoreh Deah* 264:1; *Chatham Sofer, Yoreh Deah* 31. *Hagah, Yoreh Deah* 264:1, on the other hand, ruled that drawing a drop of blood will correct the circumcision and this should be done.

CHAPTER 4

1. There are instances where the *brith* may take place immediately after the doctor determines that the child is well. In more serious illnesses, we must wait a full seven days after the child has completely recovered. See Chapter 2.

2. Rabbi M. D. Tendler cited a decision by Rabbi Moshe Feinstein in *Symposium on Medical Dilemmas and the Practise of Milah,* p. 35.

3. Ibid., p. 31.

4. Tosafoth, *Shabbath* 135a and *Yevamoth* 46b, maintains that no drop of blood is required. *Maharsha, Shabbath* 135a, explains Tosafoth by noting that since this prepuce is different from all others, it is not considered to be a prepuce. *Smag,* Negative Commandment 116, and *Yad, Hilkhoth Milah* 1:11, rule that a drop of blood must be drawn.

5. *Oth Chaim V'Shalom,* p. 248; *Zokher HaBrith,* p. 113. The *Jewish Week,* August 9, 1981, p. 23, reported that a Jewish child without a prepuce was born in Petach Tikvah on June 30, 1981, and was treated as a *nolad mahul.*

6. *Symposium,* p. 16, *Proceedings,* p. 11.

7. *Symposium,* p. 22.

8. Rabbi Moses D. Tendler in ibid., p. 29. See *Chagigah* 4a; *Yevamoth* 72a, s.v. *Mibachutz; Yad, T'rumoth* 7:14; *Sha'agath Aryeh, Rosh Hashanah* 104; *Turai Even, Chagigah* 4a; and *Yoreh Deah* 266:10.

9. *Symposium,* p. 27; *Chagigah* 4a.

10. *Shabbath* 135a; *Yad, Hilkhot Milah* 1:11; *Tur, Orach Chaim* 331:5; *Yoreh Deah* 266:10.

11. Mishnah, *Shabbath* 137a.

12. This is in accordance with *Yoreh Deah* 262:4–6 and *Shakh* 262:11.

13. Personal communication with Rabbi Moishe Bick.

14. *Yoreh Deah* 262:7.

15. Published by Gur Aryeh Institute (Brooklyn, 1967).

16. Mishnah, *Niddah* 28a.

17. *Yoreh Deah* 194:10. See *Shakh* 194:10.

18. See the following for additional information: my article in *Symposium,* p. 54; *Yerushalmi, Shabbath* 19:5; *Yerushalmi, Berakhoth* 1:1; *Shabbath* 34b; Rabbainu Tam ad loc., s.v. *Safek; Shabbath* 35, 137a; *Megillah* 20b; *Pesachim* 93b; *Niddah* 28a, 53; *Berakhoth* 2b; *Yad, Shabbath* 5:4; *Kithvai Ramban,* p. 251; *Orach Chaim* 233:1, 261:1-2, 293:2; *Biur HaGra, Yoreh Deah,* 262:9; Rabbi Shneur Zalman, *Siddur Tehillath HaShem,* p. 127; Rabbi Abraham Pimental, *Minchath Cohen,* 1:1, 4, 7 and 2:2; Rabbi M. Tucazinsky, *Bain HaShemashoth,* chap. 2; Rabbi Moshe Alashkar, s. 96; Rabbi Eliezer ben Shmu'ail M'Metz, *Sefer Yerai'im* 102; *Talmudic Encyclopedia,* vol. 3, pp. 122–129; Rabbi Moshe Feinstein, *Iggroth Moshe, Orach Chaim* 97; Leo Levi, *Jewish Chrononomy,* pp. 19–23, 269–274; Hebrew section, pp. 9–45; Rabbi Moshe B. Pirutinsky, *Sefer HaBris, M'kor U'Biur Halakha,* pp. 78–104; Rabbi Y. E. Henkin, *Aiduth L'Yisrael* p. 149.

19. *Proceedings of the Symposium on Current Concepts in Pediatrics and Urology and Their Relationship to Brith Milah,* p. 31.

20. *Symposium,* p. 40.

21. Ibid., p. 43.

22. *Hagah, Yoreh Deah* 263:5; *Zikhron Brith L'Rishonim,* p. 92; *Brith Olam,* p. 68; *Sefer HaBris,* p. 128. See *Orach Chaim* 526:9 on removal of the prepuce and burial on holidays. See also *Symposium,* p. 43.

23. *Dorland's Illustrated Medical Dictionary,* 25th ed., p. 69.

24. *Encyclopaedia Britannica,* vol. 11, p. 350.

25. Mishnah, *Yevamoth* 8:1 (70a) in accordance with Rashi's interpretation.

26. *Yevamoth* 64b; *Shabbath* 134a; *Tosafoth, Zevachim* 74b, s.v. *V'ha*; *Tosafoth, Chullin* 4b, s.v. *Sh'maithu.*

27. *Yoreh Deah* 263:2-3; *Shakh;* loc. cit.; *Tashbatz* 3:207; *Chatham Sofer, Yoreh Deah* 243; *Avnai Nezer* 324, 325, 327; *Yeshuoth Malko, Yoreh Deah* 47, 49; *Ridbaz* 13; *Chazon Ish, Yoreh Deah* 154; article by Dr. Jacob Levy in *Noam,* vol. 10; *Sefer HaBris* 263:6-27; *Nodah B'Yehudah, Yoreh Deah* 165; *Arukh HaShulchan* 263:6-11; *Brith Olam,* p. 122.

28. Rabbi Moses D. Tendler in *Proceedings,* p. 24. An infant may be afflicted with other diseases that were not discussed by the rabbis. The physician is the only one who can determine whether the child is sick. See the article by Dr. Abraham Steinberg in *Assia,* vol. 8, no. 1-2, pp. 21-44.

29. William J. Williams, M.D., *Hematology* (New York: McGraw-Hill Book Co., 1977), 2nd ed., p. 1415.

CHAPTER 5

1. *Hagah, Yoreh Deah* 263:5. The *Sif'thai Cohen,* ad loc., rules that a *mohel* may operate on a non-Jew when the circumcision is medically indicated. See *Avodah Zarah* 26b. Modern-day *mohelim* refrain from performing circumcisions on Christians because in doing so they would not be fulfilling a religious rite but, rather, performing surgery, and this should only be done by a surgeon.

2. The circumcision of a proselyte will be discussed in Chapter 7.

3. *Kiddushin* 66b and 68b; Rashi, *Bekhoroth* 47a, s.v. De'ovar; *Yad, Issurai Bi'ah* 15:3; *Even HaEzer* 4:19.

4. *Yoreh Deah* 268:6.

5. This is generally done in this manner: The father enters the ritual bath (*mikvah*) with the baby in his arms and lowers the child into the water for a second.

6. *L'Eylah* (London), Autumn 1979, pp. 8 f.

7. *Sanhedrin* 19b; *Megillah* 13a; *Yad, Ishuth* 23:17-18; *Pitchai T'shuvah, Even HaEzer* 19; *Choshen Mishpat* 60:2-5; *Responsa Rashba* 38; *Responsa Radbaz* 1:123; *Chatham Sofer, Even HaEzer* 76. Rabbi Samuel b. Nachmani said: "A person who rears an orphan boy or an orphan girl in his home and enables them to marry fulfills the verse, 'Happy are they who keep justice, and do righteousness at all times.'" This text is found in *Kethuboth* 50a on Psalm 106:3.

8. Maharsha on *Sanhedrin* 19b. See *Iggroth Moshe, Yoreh Deah* 162.

9. *Sanhedrin* 19b; *Megillah* 13a; *Even HaEzer* 114; *Choshen Mishpat* 60:2-5;

Hagah, Choshen Mishpat 42:15; *Chatham Sofer, Even HaEzer,* s. 76. There are three articles in *Noam* 4 (1961): Rudner, p. 61; Findling, p. 65; and Ezrachi, p. 94.

CHAPTER 6

1. *Orach Chaim* 559:7; *Hagah, Yoreh Deah* 265:4.

2. *Hagah, Orach Chaim* 621:3. The *Arukh HaShulchan* 621:3, however, maintains that young children may drink the wine on Yom Kippur as they do on all other fast-days. Rabbi Yosef Caro maintains that on Yom Kippur we refrain from saying the blessing on wine.

3. *Orach Chaim* 559:8.

4. *Hagah, Orach Chaim* 551:9.

5. *Orach Chaim* 686:2.

6. *B'air Haitev, Orach Chaim* 559:15. There is a view that the father of the infant may pray the Afternoon Service and need not complete the fast, for this is his festive day. See Tosafoth, *Eruvin* 40b, s.v. *Dil'ma; Orach Chaim* 559:9.

7. *Hagah, Orach Chaim* 686:2; *Sha'ar HaTziyun; Mishnah B'rurah,* loc. cit., s.k. 14, maintains that the participants fast together with the Household of Israel and enjoy the meal after sundown.

8. *Orach Chaim* 131:3; *Hagah,* loc. cit., maintains that *Tachanun* is omitted only in the synagogue where the *Brith Milah* takes place. In other synagogues within the same city, the *Tachanun* is said. *Atereth Z'kainim* on *Orach Chaim* 331:4 rules that the *Tachanun* is omitted throughout the city because Elijah the Prophet is visiting the community in honor of the brith. *Migdal Oz* (Emden), p. 15, says that each city should follow its own custom. See Rabbi Jacob Werdiger, *Aiduth L'Yisrael,* p. 134.

9. A person is an *onen* when one of seven relatives passes away: father, mother, wife, brother, sister, son, or daughter.

10. The *mohel* is different from the father, because the *mohel's* obligation is to bury his own dead, whereas the father has the added responsibility of having his son circumcised. This is inferred from *Chatham Sofer, Yoreh Deah* 325. In Rabbi Moshe Sofer's *Likutai Sha'aloth U't'shuvoth* 6:39, the ruling is expressly stated.

11. *Zokhair HaBrith,* p. 65.

12. Ibid., p. 66.

13. *Brith Olam,* p. 87.

14. Ibid., p. 83.

CHAPTER 7

1. *Yevamoth* 47b. The *mikvah* is a ritual bath. The text for the ritual of conversion is found in Chapter 12.

2. Rabbi Aryeh Kaplan, *The Handbook of Jewish Thought* (New York: Maznaim, 1979), p. 63. A sacrifice was also required of the Jews in the wilderness. See *Kerithoth* 9a; *Yad, Issurai Bi'ah* 13:1. We are permitted to convert today, even though there is no sacrifice, because of the text "Throughout your generations" (Numbers 15:14).

3. *Yevamoth* 47a; *Yoreh Deah* 268:2; *Yad, Issurai Bi'ah* 14:1-6.

4. *Shabbath* 137b, *Yoreh Deah* 264:5.

5. *Zikhron Brith L'Rishonim*, p. 135.

6. *Pesachim* 7b; Tosafoth, loc. cit., s.v. *Al HaTvilah*; *Berakhoth* 51a; Rashi, loc. cit., s.v. *Hassam*; *Yevamoth* 47b; *Yoreh Deah* 268:2.

7. *Yoreh Deah* 268:3.

8. *Yoreh Deah* 268:7.

9. Exodus 18:12, which the rabbis interpret as a *Seudath Mitzvah* after Jethro was converted to Judaism. See *Torah Sh'laimah*, loc. cit.

CHAPTER 8

1. *Baba Kama* 80a.

2. Rabbainu Tam, loc. cit., s.v. *L'vai*; Rashi, s.v. *Yeshua Haben*, interprets this term as the *Pidyon Haben*, the Redemption of the First-Born.

3. *T'rumath HaDeshen* 269.

4. *Hagah, Yoreh Deah* 265:12; *Taz* 265:13.

5. *Midrash Rabbah Leviticus* 27:10. The Sabbath is known as the Sabbath Queen. Before entering into a covenantal relationship with God, respect must first be given to the Sabbath Queen.

6. Rashi, *Baba Bathra* 60b.

7. *Torath HaAdam* 109. Rabbi Chavel in his commentary suggests that a festive meal be held when the baby girl is seven days old.

8. Jerusalem Talmud, *Kethuboth* 1:5.

9. *Hagah, Yoreh Deah* 265:5, and *Shakh* 265:21.

10. *Zikhron Brith L'Rishonim* 61. It is not being suggested that this custom be revived, but it is noted here to recall how difficult it was at times to fulfill the word of God in face of intolerable oppression.

11. *Shibalai HaLeket, Hilkhoth Milah*, 4.

12. *Zikhron Brith L'Rishonim* 62 ff.

13. Exodus 15:2.

14. *Shabbath* 133b.

15. Loc. cit., s.v. *D'lo*.

16. *Shakh, Yoreh Deah* 265:24, citing the *Hagaoth Minhagim*, says that this is based on the fact that the *milah* is an *oth*, a "sign," and that Tephillin, too, is an *oth*; consequently they go well together.

17. *Sandek* will be defined below in the text.

18. *Yoreh Deah* 265:6.

19. Ibid. 265:11.

20. *Magen Avraham, Orach Chaim* 551:3. *Zokher HaBrith* 62 and *Brith Olam* 177. The woman is called *kvaterin*, and the man is the *kvater*.

21. *Machzor Vitry*, pt. 2, 505. *Haba* numerically equals eight, alluding to the eight-day-old boy who is to be circumcised. The assemblage remains standing in accordance with 2 Kings 23:3, "everyone stood at the *brith.*"

22. Genesis 17:12.

23. *Yoreh Deah* 265:11; *Zokher HaBrith* 20:1.

24. *Milon Chadash*, p. 1108; *Arukh HaShalaim*, vol. 6, p. 83. *Yalkut Shimoni*, Psalm 72, refers to this word as *sandikus*.

25. *Responsa Rabbi Akiva Eiger* 42.

26. *Brith Olam*, p. 197.

27. *Hagah, Yoreh Deah* 265:11.

28. *Shila, Chullin* 113b.

29. *Yoreh Deah* 265:9, derived from *Taanith* 27a, rhetorically asks, "Is it possible that a person's sacrifice be offered and the donor should not be present?"

30. *Yoreh Deah* 265:12; *Hagah*, loc. cit. It is a *Seudath Mitzvah* because it is a meal that is associated with a good deed. Rif and Rosh, *Pesachim* 109a.

31. *Yad, Hilkhoth Yom Tov* 6:18.

32. *Magen Avraham, Orach Chaim* 568:9 and 559:11; *Orach Chaim* 588:10. See Chapter 6.

33. *Hagah, Orach Chaim* 249:2.

34. *Responsa of Tashbatz* 3:8.

35. *Arukh HaShulchan, Yoreh Deah* 265:16.

36. *Hagah, Yoreh Deah* 265:1. *Orach Chaim* 213 concurs.

37. *Arukh HaShulchan, Yoreh Deah* 265:13. This is based on the *Siddur* of Saadia Gaon.

38. *Hagaoth Smak* 157; *Arukh HaShulchan, Even HaEzer* 62:10.

39. *Hagah, Yoreh Deah* 265:1; *Responsa of Rabbi Akiva Eiger* 42.

40. *Yoreh Deah* 265:7.

41. *Hagah, Yoreh Deah* 265:7 and *Shakh* 265:17.

42. Ibid., s.k. 15–16.

43. *Yoreh Deah* 265:5 and *Hagah*, loc. cit. *Hagah* permits the saying of the blessing for two children whether they are twins or children of different parents. At a marriage ceremony we never have one service for two couples. See *Hagah, Even HaEzer* 61:3.

CHAPTER 9

1. Genesis 17:1–12.

2. Genesis 17:14.

3. Genesis 17:19.

4. Genesis 21:4.

5. Exodus 4:25–26.

6. Exodus 12:48.

7. Leviticus 12:3.

8. Leviticus 26:9.

9. Joshua 5:2–7. The reason for abstaining from the *Brith Milah* in the wilderness was stated in Chapter 1.

10. 1 Kings 19:10.

11. Jeremiah 14:21.

12. Jeremiah 32:40.

13. Jeremiah 33:25.

14. Jeremiah 34:10.

15. Jeremiah 50:5.

16. Isaiah 54:10.

17. Isaiah 59:21.

18. Ezekiel 16:6.

19. Zechariah 9:11.

20. Psalm 74:20.

21. Psalm 105:8–10.

22. Psalm 106:45.

23. Psalm 111:5.

24. *Genesis Rabbah* 42:8.

25. *Pirkai Rabbi Eliezer,* chap. 28. Most commentators maintain that Abraham circumcised himself. This is the view of Rashi and the Ramban on Genesis 17:24. See *Genesis Rabbah* 42:9.

25ᵃ. *Nedarim* 32a.

26. Jeremiah 33:25; *Nedarim* 31b.

27. *Pirkai Rabbi Eliezer,* chap. 28.

28. Ibid.

29. *Tanchuma, Shemini* 8.

30. Mishnah, *Nedarim* 31b. In Genesis 17, where the command was given to Abraham to circumcise himself, the word *brith* appears thirteen times. Maimonides lists these thirteen times in his commentary to the Mishnah and in his *Yad* at the end of *Hilkhoth Milah.*

31. *Nedarim* 31b. We are, therefore, permitted to perform a *brith* on the Sabbath.

32. Ibid.

33. *Nedarim* 32a.

34. *Menachoth* 43b.

35. *Shabbath* 130a. See *Rosh Hashanah* 19a. A similar decree was ordered by Antiochus, the Syrian king; see *Scroll of the Hasmoneans* 1:9–10.

36. *Megillah* 16b, referring to Esther 8:16.
37. *Shabbath* 130a.
38. *Pirkai Rabbi Eliezer,* chap. 28, and *Zohar, Tazria.*
39. *Tanchuma, Lekh*; Exodus 19:5.
40. *Yalkut Shimoni, Tazria* 12, p. 326; Proverbs 30:5.
41. *Deuteronomy Rabbah, Ki Thaitzai.*
42. Maimonides, *Guide to the Perplexed,* edited by Yehuda Ibn Shmuel (Jerusalem: Mossad Harav Kook, 1946), p. 170. Physicians offer additional reasons for the eighth day. For example, Dr. Charles Schlosberg says: "Circumcision at eight days of age, as in the Jewish ritual practice, seems preferable as this gives the child a chance to reach general physiologic homeostasis following birth; also, during this time contraindicating conditions will usually manifest themselves." *Clinical Pediatrics,* April 1971, p. 207. Dr. Elliot Leiter suggested the same reasons in a personal communication to this writer. Moreover, according to Dr. Gerhart S. Schwarz, "This [the eighth day] is exactly the day on which the blood clotting faculty of the baby reaches the adult level" *Bulletin of the New York Academy of Medicine* 57, no. 9 (November 1981): 820.
43. *Tanchuma,* ed. Buber, Leviticus 22:27, ii, 94.
44. *Guide to the Perplexed,* p. 568.
45. *The Pentateuch: Translation and Commentary by Rabbi Samson R. Hirsch,* rendered into English by Isaac Levy, 2nd ed., vol. 1, p. 301.

CHAPTER 10

1. The Maharam of Rothenburg, *Responsa* 504, wrote that the practice that all rise and remain standing throughout the circumcision service is derived from "everyone stood at the *brith*" (2 Kings 23:3). The *sandek,* however, sits in order to hold the baby, so *Bikkurim* 3:3; *Machzor Vitry,* p. 627; *Ba'al Yosef Umetz* 325.

Standing is a way of paying respect to the baby and serving as a welcome to Elijah. Elijah or his representative is spiritually present at every *Brith Milah.* We pray silently that he will guard and guide the child. The word *haba* is the acronym for *hinai ba Eliyahu,* "Behold! Elijah is coming." *Haba* numerically equals eight, or the eighth day, when the child is circumcised.

2. Genesis 17:12. This formula is also recited before performing other *mitzvoth.*

3. Two chairs are in readiness—one for Elijah and one for the *sandek.*

4. Genesis 49:18; Psalms 119:166, 162, 165; 65:5. The last verse is divided in two. The first part is said by the *mohel* and the second by all present. This is based on the *Zohar, Lekh Lekha.* See *Taz, Yoreh Deah* 265:12.

5. The text for this blessing is given in *Menachoth* 42a; *Shabbath* 137b; Jerusalem Talmud, *Berakhoth* 9:3. Maimonides in *Yad, Hilkhoth Milah* 3:1, rules that when the father is the *mohel,* the text should be emended to *lamul eth haben. Yoreh Deah* 265:2 offers the decision of Maimonides. *Hagah,* loc. cit., gives the Ashkenazic practice of reciting the same text whether the father or a *mohel* is the circumciser.

6. This is not an additional blessing for the *brith.* It is a pledge that the father will rear the child properly and fulfill all the *mitzvoth* incumbent on him. See Tosafoth, *Shabbath* 137b, s.v. *Avi,* and *Rosh, Shabbath* 19:10. Should the father serve as the *mohel,* he recites both blessings—this one and the one usually said by the *mohel*—before the circumcision. See the comment of *Taz* on *Yoreh Deah* 265:1 and *Chakhmath Adam* 149:20.

7. *Shabbath* 137b.

8. The Talmud does not require that wine be used at the *brith.* Other liquids are acceptable. Should another liquid be used, the *she'hakol* blessing is recited. It is customary to dip gauze into the cup with the liquid and then dab the baby's lips with it. See *Or Zarua* 2:107; Tosafoth, *Eruvin* 40b, s.v. *Dilma; P'air Hador* 93. *Magen Avraham, Orach Chaim* 174:17, states that we do not say *savri* at a *brith.*

9. Rashi identifies the "beloved person" as Isaac, *Shabbath* 137b, s.v. *Asher.* Rabbainu Tam says that this refers to Isaac, loc. cit., s.v. *Y'did.* The *Arukh,* s.v. *Y'did,* maintains that Jacob is meant. *Zikhron Brith L'Rishonim,* p. 89, states that the *Arukh* concurs with the view of Rav Hai Gaon. Undoubtedly all the Patriarchs were "beloved persons." The *mohel* prays that the baby be spared all the days of his life and in the hereafter.

10. The *mohel* offers another prayer for the child. See *Midrash Sekhel Tov* 1:19a and *Targum Yonathan ben Uziel* on Genesis 48:20. When twins are circumcised with one ceremony, the plural form is used, i.e., *kayaim eth ha'yeladim l'avihem ul'imam; Hagah, Yoreh Deah* 265:5.

11. The Biblical verses in this prayer include Proverbs 23:25, Ezekiel 16:6, Psalm 105:8–10, Genesis 21:4 and Psalm 118:1.

12. *Zikhron Brith L'Rishonim,* p. 97, explains "soaking in your blood" in accordance with *Pirkai Rabbi Eliezer* 48:89. Since the Egyptians did not provide straw to make the bricks (Exodus 5:7), our ancestors fetched it in the wilderness. The straw was thorny, and during the gathering they would get bruised and their blood would flow. This blood mingled with the straw and became part of the bricks.

There is a custom to say the *Alenu* and the *Kaddish* at the conclusion of the *Brith Milah;* see *Shakh, Yoreh Deah* 265:24.

CHAPTER 11

1. *Chullin* 105a; *Sotah* 4b; Yerushalmi, *Berakhoth* 8:2; *Orach Chaim* 158:1.

2. *Berakhoth* 35a.

3. The author of this *piyut* was Rabbi Judah HaLevi. It is included in the service of the seventh day of Passover. Many communities chant this religious poem at every *brith*. The text is as follows:

יוֹם לְיַבָּשָׁה, נֶהֶפְכוּ מְצוּלִים. שִׁירָה חֲדָשָׁה, שִׁבְּחוּ גְאוּלִים: הִטְבַּעְתָּ בְּתַרְמִית. רַגְלֵי בַת עֲנָמִית. וּפַעֲמֵי שֻׁלַמִּית. יָפוּ בַנְּעָלִים. שִׁירָה חדשה שבחו גאולים: וְכָל רוֹאֵי יְשָׁרוּן. בְּבֵית הוֹדִי, יְשׁוֹרְרוּן. אֵין כָּאֵל יְשָׁרוּן. וְאוֹיְבֵינוּ פְּלִילִים. שִׁירָה חדשה שבחו גאולים: דְּגָלֵי בֶן תָּרִים. עַל הַנִּשְׁאָרִים. וּתְלַקֵּט נִפְזָרִים. כִּמְלַקֵּט שִׁבֳּלִים. שִׁירָה חדשה שבחו גאולים: הַבָּאִים עִמְּךָ בִּבְרִית חוֹתָמָךְ. וּמִבֶּטֶן לְשִׁמָךְ. הֵמָּה נִמּוֹלִים. שִׁירָה חדשה שבחו גאולים: הַרְאֵה אוֹתוֹתָם. לְכָל רוֹאֵי אוֹתָם. וְעַל כַּנְפֵי כְסוּתָם. יַעֲשׂוּ גְדִילִים. שִׁירָה חדשה שבחו גאולים: לְמִי זֹאת נִרְשֶׁמֶת. הַבֵּר נָא דְבַר אֱמֶת. לְמִי הַחוֹתֶמֶת, וּלְמִי הַפְּתִילִים. שִׁירָה חדשה שבחו גאולים: וְשׁוּב שֵׁנִית לְקַדְּשָׁהּ. וְאַל תּוֹסִיף לְגָרְשָׁהּ. וְהַעֲלֵה אוֹר שִׁמְשָׁהּ. וְנָסוּ הַצְּלָלִים. שִׁירָה חדשה שבחו גאולים: יְדִידִים רוֹמְמוּךָ. בְּשִׁירָה קִדְּמוּךָ. מִי כָמֹכָה. יְיָ, בָּאֵלִים. שִׁירָה חֲדָשָׁה, שִׁבְּחוּ גְאוּלִים:

4. The saying of grace after meals is implicit in the verse "You shall eat and be satisfied and bless . . ." (Deuteronomy 8:10). See *Berakhoth* 48b.

5. Individuals who introduce the Grace with Psalm 137 on weekdays, may say it at a Pidyon Haben. See *Tz'lotha D'Avraham*, p. 495. The following is the text of Psalm 137:

עַל נַהֲרוֹת בָּבֶל שָׁם יָשַׁבְנוּ גַּם בָּכִינוּ, בְּזָכְרֵנוּ אֶת צִיּוֹן. עַל עֲרָבִים בְּתוֹכָהּ, תָּלִינוּ כִּנֹּרוֹתֵינוּ. כִּי שָׁם, שְׁאֵלוּנוּ שׁוֹבֵינוּ דִּבְרֵי שִׁיר, וְתוֹלָלֵינוּ שִׂמְחָה; שִׁירוּ לָנוּ מִשִּׁיר צִיּוֹן. אֵיךְ נָשִׁיר אֶת שִׁיר יְיָ עַל אַדְמַת נֵכָר. אִם אֶשְׁכָּחֵךְ יְרוּשָׁלַיִם, תִּשְׁכַּח יְמִינִי: תִּדְבַּק לְשׁוֹנִי לְחִכִּי, אִם לֹא אֶזְכְּרֵכִי, אִם לֹא אַעֲלֶה אֶת יְרוּשָׁלַיִם, עַל רֹאשׁ שִׂמְחָתִי: זְכֹר יְיָ לִבְנֵי אֱדוֹם, אֵת יוֹם יְרוּשָׁלָיִם; הָאוֹמְרִים עָרוּ עָרוּ עַד הַיְסוֹד בָּהּ. בַּת בָּבֶל הַשְּׁדוּדָה אַשְׁרֵי שֶׁיְשַׁלֶּם לָךְ, אֶת גְּמוּלֵךְ, שֶׁגָּמַלְתְּ לָנוּ: אַשְׁרֵי שֶׁיֹּאחֵז וְנִפֵּץ אֶת עֹלָלַיִךְ, אֶל הַסָּלַע.

6. *Chullin* 105a; *Orach Chaim* 181:1.

7. *Hagah, Orach Chaim* 182:1.

8. Psalm 34:4, *Pesachim* 103b.

9. *Magen Avraham, Orach Chaim* 192:1.

10. Tosafoth, *Berakhoth* 47a, s.v. *V'hilkhatha;* Werdiger, op. cit., p. 499. *Berakhoth* 50a, *Orach Chaim* 192:1.

11. Mishnah, *Berakhoth* 49b.

12. This prayer was composed by Moses (ca. 1220 B.C.E.) in thankfulness for the manna (Exodus 16:1–36) which the Eternal rained down from heaven to provide sustenance for the Israelites in the wilderness. See *Berakhoth* 48b. The

second blessing, "We thank You" (*Nodeh L'kha*) and "We acclaim You," (*V'al Hakol*), was written by Joshua (ca. 1170 B.C.E.) after the conquest of the land of Israel. The third prayer, "Have mercy" (*Rachaim*), was written by David (ca. 1006 B.C.E.) and Solomon (ca. 933 B.C.E.). These three prayers constitute the essential part of the Grace.

A fourth prayer, "Who showers kindness" (*Hatov V'hamaitiv*), was composed in Yavneh when permission was granted to bury the massacred Jewish soldiers in Bethar (135 C.E.). Rabban Gamaliel and his rabbinic court fasted, prayed, and gave their possessions to the Roman conquerors in order to obtain permission to bury the dead. See Tosafoth, *Pesachim* 104b, s.v. *Hatov*; *Taanith* 31a; and *Gittin* 57a.

Additional prayers were subsequently added to mark special occasions. These are discussed below.

13. This is the second prayer, and it was written by Joshua, as was noted above. The standard formula of *Barukh Ata* at the opening and conclusion is omitted because of the rule of "a blessing that is close to another blessing"; see *Yad, Hilkhoth Berakhoth* 11:1.

14. *Shabbath* 24a states that the miracle of Chanukah should be recalled together with the "Thank" benediction. See Rashi, loc. cit., s.v. *B'hoda'ah*, and Tosafoth, s.v. *Mazkir*; *Hagah, Orach Chaim* 682:1.

15. The miracle of Purim is in the same category as Chanukah.

16. This prayer of thanksgiving is based on Deuteronomy 8:10. See Rashi, *Berakhoth* 49a, s.v. *T'chila V'sof*, and *B'air Haitev, Orach Chaim* 187:1.

17. This is the third blessing, as was noted above (note 12). The reference to Jerusalem was added by David; Solomon expressed his thanksgiving for being privileged to erect the Temple. See *Berakhoth* 48b.

18. The sages say that the prayer for the Sabbath must be said between the consolation prayer "Have mercy" (*Rachaim*) and the prayer for the rebuilding of Jerusalem (*U'v'nai*), which is also a prayer of consolation; *Berakhoth* 48b. See the commentary of *Leviticus Rabbah* 34:15 on Isaiah 58:11. See also *Orach Chaim* 188:8.

19. This prayer may be required at a *Brith Milah*. At a *Pidyon Haben* it is said only during the Intermediate Days of Pesach, Sukkoth, and Rosh Chodesh. It was placed in this position because it is a prayer. See Tosafoth, *Shabbath* 24a, s.v. *B'vonai*.

20. *Berakhoth* 49a.

21. This is the fourth blessing, referred to in note 12. See *Berakhoth* 48b; Tosafoth, *Pesachim* 104a, s.v. *Hatov*; *Taanith* 31a; *Baba Bathra* 121b; *Gittin* 57a.

22. *Baba Bathra* 17a.

Where applicable, prayers may be offered for one's family and for parents. These are the texts:

הָרַחֲמָן, הוּא יְבָרֵךְ אוֹתִי (וְאֶת אִשְׁתִּי וְאֶת זַרְעִי) וְאֶת כָּל אֲשֶׁר לִי.

הָרַחֲמָן, הוּא יְבָרֵךְ—אֶת (אָבִי מוֹרִי) בַּעַל הַבַּיִת הַזֶּה, וְאֶת (אִמִּי מוֹרָתִי) בַּעֲלַת הַבַּיִת הַזֶּה,
אוֹתָם וְאֶת בֵּיתָם וְאֶת זַרְעָם וְאֶת כָּל אֲשֶׁר לָהֶם—אוֹתָנוּ וְאֶת כָּל אֲשֶׁר לָנוּ. כְּמוֹ שֶׁנִּתְבָּרְכוּ אֲבוֹתֵינוּ
אַבְרָהָם יִצְחָק וְיַעֲקֹב: בַּכֹּל מִכֹּל כֹּל. כֵּן יְבָרֵךְ אוֹתָנוּ כֻּלָּנוּ יַחַד. בִּבְרָכָה שְׁלֵמָה, וְנֹאמַר אָמֵן.

23. These prayers are attributed to Rabbi Abraham ben Isaac HaCohen.

24. This prayer is not applicable at a *Pidyon Haben,* since the latter is never conducted on a Sabbath or holy day. A *Pidyon Haben* may take place on Rosh Chodesh and the Intermediate Days of Pesach and Sukkoth. *Tamid* 33b interprets Psalm 92, which is chanted on the Sabbath, as referring to the time of eternal rest and peace.

25. This is based on Amos 9:11.

26. This verse is found in Psalm 18:51 and 2 Samuel 22:51. Each, however, has a slightly different reading. The Psalmist renders *magdil* and Samuel has *migdol.* One reading was assigned to weekdays and one to the Sabbath and festivals.

27. Psalms 34:10–11, 118:1, 145:16; Jeremiah 17:7; Psalms 37:25, 29:11.

28. *Pesachim* 103b and Tosafoth, loc. cit., s.v. *Rav Ashi.* See *Orach Chaim* 190:4.

29. Works that may be consulted for further information on the liturgy include: *Tz'lotha D'Avraham* by Rabbi Abraham Landau and his grandson Rabbi Menachem Mendel Landau, (2 vols.), printed in Israel by the Institute for Research of Jewish Liturgy, 1963; *Otzar Hatfiloth* by Aryeh Leib ben Shlomo Gordon and Chanokh Zundel ben Yosef, republished in New York, 1946; *Machzor Vitry* by Rabbi Simcha ben Samuel of Vitry, ed. by S. Hurwitz, 1889–93; *Siddur Ha'Gra* by Rabbi Elijah ben Solomon, the Gaon of Vilna, republished in Jerusalem, 1895; *Avodath Yisrael* by Rabbi Isaac Seligman Baer, 1868; *Tehillath HaShem,* reprinted in New York with an English translation, 1978. This *Siddur* was originally prepared by Rabbi Shneur Zalman of Liadi and published in Kapust, 1816. The *Siddur* of Rabbi Yaakov of Emden, *Beth Yaakov,* was referred to earlier. Two popular translations of the *Siddur* include S. Singer, *The Authorized Daily Prayer Book,* published in 1890, and P. Birnbaum, *Daily Prayer Book,* published in 1949. Both of these works have appeared in numerous editions. For a guide to Jewish prayer, the reader may see *To Pray as a Jew* by Rabbi Hayim H. Donin (New York: Basic Books, 1980). A translation of the *Siddur* is offered by Rabbi Ben Zion Bokser in his *Prayer Book* (New York: Hebrew Publishing Co., 1957, 1961).

CHAPTER 12

1. *Shabbath* 137b, *Yoreh Deah* 268:5. In instances where the prospective

proselyte has already been circumcised before converting to Judaism, a drop of blood is drawn but no blessings are said. See *Yoreh Deah* 268:1.

2. Jeremiah 33:25.

3. This blessing is added in accordance with the *Taz* 268, s.k. 12.

4. The prayer for the welfare of the proselyte is found in *Zikhron Brith L'Rishonim*, p. 135. Note that it is similar in many respects to the prayer offered for an infant during *Brith Milah*.

5. Psalm 118:1.

CHAPTER 13

1. Exodus 13:2.

2. Rashi on Numbers 8:17; *Tanchuma*, Numbers 8:6, Numbers 3:13. *Minchath Shmu'ail* in *She'eltoth De Rav Ahai Gaon*, vol. 5, p. 3; and Rabbi Abraham Sperling, *Ta'amai HaMinhagim Umkorai Hadinim*, p. 397.

3. *Zevachim* 112b (14:4).

4. Exodus 32:26, *Yoma* 66b.

5. Numbers 3:39 states that there were 22,000 Levites, and Numbers 3:43 notes that there were 22,273 first-born sons. There was an excess of 273 first-born. See *Emek Davar*, Numbers 3:41.

6. The plural of shekel is *shekalim* in Hebrew.

7. Numbers 3:46–51.

8. Separate chapters will be devoted to the ceremony and to the definition of shekel and of the thirty-first day of the baby.

9. *Bekhoroth* 49b; *Kiddushin* 29a; *Yad, Hilkhoth Bekhorim* 11:1; *Chakhmath Adam* 150:1.

10. See Chapter 14 for additional exceptions.

11. *Sefer HaChinukh*, p. 63, writes that this is to remind us that everything belongs to God.

12. Rabbi Samuel R. Hirsch, *The Pentateuch: Translated and Explained*, rendered into English by Isaac Levy, 2d ed. (New York: Judaica Press, 1971), vol. 2, p. 162.

13. *Chatham Sofer, Yoreh Deah* 134. Rabbi Yaakov of Emden, *Beth Yaakov*, p. 104, maintains that this amount is to atone for the selling of Joseph by his brothers for twenty pieces of silver, which is the equivalent of five shekels.

14. *Arukh HaShulchan, Yoreh Deah* 305:36.

CHAPTER 14

1. Mishnah, *Bekhoroth* 46a, and *Yoreh Deah* 305:17.

2. Exodus 13:2; Mishnah, *Bekhoroth* 13a, 47a; *Chullin* 132a and Tosafoth, s.v. *Rav Kahana,* and Rosh, loc. cit. The son of a *Levi*'s daughter is exempt from redemption, but subsequent generations are Israelites and require redemption.

3. This is based on Numbers 3:45, "Take the Levites [which actually refers to Levites and *Cohanim*] in place of the first-born among the people of Israel." In other words, the redemption in the wilderness was accomplished by the *Cohen* or *Levi* accepting the holiness of the first-born. This was the only time that a *Levi* could redeem a *bekhor* (Numbers 3:39). See *Bekhoroth* 4a, 47a; *Arukh HaShulchan, Yoreh Deah* 305:56.

4. *Chakhmath Adam* 150.

5. *Ikrai Dinim* 33:36 cites *Pri HaAretz* 18 that this child is in a class by itself (*sui generis*). This is in accordance with Mishnah, *Bekhoroth* 41a. See also *Baba Bathra* 126b, 140b; *Shabbath* 134b; *Yad, Erekhin* 1:5, and *Yoreh Deah* 315:2–3.

6. *Bekhoroth* 42b, *Yoreh Deah* 315:2.

7. *Yoreh Deah* 305:23, *Chakhmath Adam* 150. There are authorities who maintain that we cannot always make a definite determination as to the age of the fetus, and they advise that the redemption take place but the blessings be omitted, thus avoiding using His name in vain. In such instances, the *Cohen* should return the five shekels. *Chatham Sofer, Yoreh Deah* 199, maintains that should the mother have another baby after losing the fetus, the *Cohen* may say the blessing "who granted us life" (*She'he'che'yanu*) if the father insists that he keep the five shekels. See *Mahrik* 143, *She'iltoth Yavetz* 1:49, *Nodah B'Yehuda Tenyana* 188.

8. *Williams' Obstetrics,* p. 305.

9. *Bekhoroth* 46a.

10. *Choshen Mishpat* 277:12.

11. *Zokher HaBrith,* p. 176, no. 15.

12. Ibid., no. 16. See *Kuntrath HaSfaikoth* 6:5, citing the *Tzemach Tzedek.* See article by Rabbi Pesach Y. Yavrov in *Noam,* vol. 20, pp. 279–287. These rulings are based on *Taharoth* 4:12.

13. Mishnah, *Bekhoroth* 46a; *Yoreh Deah* 305:20. The *Arukh HaShulchan, Yoreh Deah* 305:62, explains that the Torah's emphasis was on *peter rechem b'Yisrael.* The essential thing was that the mother's womb was opened when she was Jewish, and following conversion she is, of course, Jewish. Rabbi Moshe Feinstein, op. cit., *siman* 194, does not agree that the redemption money is required, but he states that it may be given.

14. *Yoreh Deah* 305:21.

15. Exodus 13:2. *Bekhoroth* 19a and 47b; *Yad, Hilkhoth Bekhorim* 2:4; *Yoreh Deah* 305:24 and 315:2.

16. Mishnah, *Bekhoroth* 49a; *Baba Kama* 11b; *Yoreh Deah* 305:12; *Arukh HaShulchan, Yoreh Deah* 305:47.

CHAPTER 15

1. *Kiddushin* 29a; *Yoreh Deah* 305:1; *Yad, Hilkhoth Bekhorim* 11:1; *Arukh HaShulchan, Yoreh Deah* 305:4; *Sefer HaChinukh,* p. 494.

2. *P'nai Maivin* on *Yoreh Deah* 226 as cited by *Aiduth L'Yisrael,* p. 154. See *Maharach, Orach Chaim* 11.

3. *Arukh HaShulchan, Yoreh Deah* 305:10.

4. *Arugath HaBosem, Yoreh Deah* 240.

5. *Responsa Imrai Yosher* 1:186.

6. *Hagah, Yoreh Deah* 305:10; *Chut Hashaini* 92, cited in *Pitchai T'shuvah* 305:1; *Chakham Tzvi* 92 maintains that we may force the father to redeem his son.

7. *Shakh, Yoreh Deah* 305:11; *Chatham Sofer, Yoreh Deah* 297.

8. The ruling is that a messenger is like the man himself (*Kiddushin* 41b). Consequently, many authorities maintain that the father may delegate a messenger to act in his place. *Chatham Sofer, Yoreh Deah* 294–295, says that it is preferable for the father to observe the rite at a distant place rather than designate a messenger.

9. *Hagah, Yoreh Deah* 305:10. See *Responsa Maharam Shik, Orach Chaim* 53; *Maharam Mintz* 1:15; and *Chatham Sofer, Yoreh Deah* 292.

10. *Kiddushin* 29a; *Yad, Bekhorim* 11:2; *Smak,* Positive Commandment 144; *Or Zarua, Hilkhoth Bekhoroth* 514; *Yoreh Deah* 305:15.

11. *Kiddushin* 29a; *Yoreh Deah* 305:15.

CHAPTER 16

1. Mishnah, *Bekhoroth* 49a; *Yoreh Deah* 305:11; *Menachoth* 37a and Tosafoth. loc. cit., s.v. *Shomea.*

2. Numbers 3:40.

3. Rashi, *Bekhoroth* 49a, s.v. *Yachzir; Sefer HaChinukh,* p. 492.

4. Tosafoth, *Bekhoroth* 49a, s.v. *Meth.*

5. *Shakh, Yoreh Deah* 305:12.

6. *Magen Avraham, Orach Chaim* 339:8.

7. *Zokher HaBrith,* p. 179, no. 14.

8. *Iggroth Moshe, Yoreh Deah* 2:118.

9. *Sefer HaChinukh,* p. 493.

10. *Magen Avraham, Orach Chaim* 249:5, 568:10.

11. *T'rumath HaDeshen* 269; *Yoreh Deah* 305:11, and *Shakh,* loc. cit.; *Ribash* 157.

12. *Hagah, Yoreh Deah* 305:11; *Orach Chaim* 546:4. Other Rabbinic authorities, however, forbid having the redemption during the intermediate days of a festival due to the principle that one "rejoicing" may not be merged with another "rejoicing"; *Moed Katan* 8b and Tosafoth, loc. cit., s.v. *L'phi.* The former opinion maintains that the prohibition applies only to marriage but not to other happy occasions. See *Arukh HaShulchan* 305:46.

13. *Hagah, Orach Chaim* 696:8.

14. *Shakh, Yoreh Deah* 305:12; *Magen Avraham, Orach Chaim* 568:10; *Arukh HaShulchan* 305:45.

15. See note 14.

16. *Shakh, Yoreh Deah* 305:12.

17. *Orach Chaim* 480:1. There is an opinion that a first-born girl is also obliged to fast. But the overwhelming opinion is that a first-born girl need not fast. See *Mishnah B'rurah,* loc. cit.

CHAPTER 17

1. Rif, *Kiddushin* 6a; Rav Hai Gaon, *Mishp'tai Sh'vuoth* 1; Maimonides, *Perush HaMishnayoth, Bekhoroth* 49b. Rabbi Zvi H. Eisenstadt, "Nachmanides, His Letter About the Coin 'Shekel Israel' and Its Weight," *Talpioth,* vol. 3–4, p. 606. Occasionally merchants fashioned their own private coins (Genesis 23:16). See A. R. Burns, *Money and Monetary Policy in Early Times* (New York: Alfred A. Knopf, 1927), p. 200. The measure of an "inch" is also derived from the term *uncia.*

2. Genesis 23:16.

3. Exodus 30:13.

4. 2 Samuel 14:26. Bruno Kisch, *Scales and Weights* (New Haven: Yale University Press, 1965), p. 219, maintains that the king's weight was identical with the sanctuary weight.

5. The post-Biblical term for the sanctuary weight was *sela.* The plural form of this word is *sela'im.*

6. The coin that was current in Western Europe during the time of the *Rishonim,* the early scholars, from the beginning of the eleventh century until the end of the fifteenth century, was the "mark." There were twelve different weights and values for the mark, depending on the city where the coin was minted. See Eisenstadt, op. cit., pp. 613 f.

7. Jerusalem Talmud, *Shekalim* 1:6. This referred to the half-shekel that was to be given annually for the maintenance of the Temple in Jerusalem. See Exodus 30:13.

8. *Perush HaMishnayoth, Bekhoroth* 49b. The seed, too, varies in weight but

not as much as currency, which is subject to inflation and deflation. See *Shakh* and *Taz, Yoreh Deah* 305:1.

9. A barley seed is 0.7 of a wheat seed.

10. Eisenstadt, op. cit., p. 607.

11. This is based on the fact that a barley seed weighs 0.045 gram.

12. The difference between the two is that there are 12 troy ounces to a troy pound while the avoirdupois ounce is 16 to the pound. A troy ounce consists of 31.1035 grams and the avoirdupois ounce weighs 28.3495 grams. See *Webster's Third New International Dictionary* (Unabridged), p. 1399.

13. *Encyclopaedia Judaica,* vol. 16, cols. 378 and 384. See A. Reifenberg, *Ancient Jewish Coins* (1947); J. Fraenkel, *History of the Shekel* (1956); and M. Narkiss, *Matb'oth HaYehudim* (1936).

14. The merchant's shekel weighed approximately 10 grams. The difference in weight of well-preserved coins may be due to wear and tear which diminished the coin. The added weight may be due to oxidation or encrustation which have added to the weight. See Bruno Kisch, op. cit., p. 2.

15. *Encyclopaedia Judaica,* vol. 5, col. 706.

16. See his commentary on Exodus 21:32.

17. Eisenstadt, op. cit., p. 613. These ranged in weight from 23.20 to 29.92 grams. The Cologne mark was the standard unit of most countries in Europe up to the middle of the nineteenth century. See Kisch, op. cit., p. 224. A. E. Berriman, *Historical Metrology* (New York: Dutton, 1953), p. 137, states that "French metrology was so bedeviled by variation that Necker told Louis XVI in 1778 that no attempt to achieve uniformity would produce results proportionate to the trouble involved."

18. See his commentary on Exodus 30:13.

19. Eisenstadt, op. cit., p. 615.

20. Rabbi Charles B. Chavel, *Ramban: His Life and Teachings* (New York: Feldheim, 1960), p. 58.

21. Eisenstadt, op. cit., p. 616. Chavel, *Perush HaRamban al HaTorah, Devarim* (Jerusalem: Mossad Harav Kook, 1972), p. 507.

22. Eisenstadt, op. cit., p. 607.

23. This is the view of Rabbi Avraham I. Karelitz, *Chazon Ish, Yoreh Deah* 182:19. See also Rabbi Jacob Kanewsky, *Shiurim Shel Torah* (Tel Aviv, Eshel), p. 24; Rabbi Abraham H. Noe, *Shiurai Torah* (Jerusalem, 1946), 3, 43; and Dov Rosen, *Shema Yisrael,* p. 205. Rabbi Moshe Greenwald, *Arugas HaBosem, Yoreh Deah* 239, records that he weighed the prescribed number of 1,920 barley beans and the weight equaled 94 grams. Rabbi Yoseph E. Henkin, *Aiduth L'Yisrael,* p. 195, maintains that 100 grams of silver are required. Rabbi Hoffman, *M'lamaid l'ho'il* 2:100, says that 105 grams are needed.

24. A pamphlet entitled *Silver Content of World Coins* by S. Nelms may be purchased by writing c/o POB 633, Hicksville, N.Y. 11756.

25. *Services for the Redemption of the First Born* (London: Initiation Society, 1965), p. 4.

26. Genesis 23:15–16.

27. *Encyclopaedia Judaica,* vol. 5, col. 696.

28. *Chazon Ish,* 182:19. He bases his decision on the *Gra, Yoreh Deah* 305:4. To determine the number of grams involved, we multiply 3,000 by 19.20 grams to the shekel, and the total is 57,600 grams of silver.

The ring which the bridegroom gives to his bride takes the place of the *perutah,* or "penny," which must be transmitted in order to legalize the marriage. This "penny" contained one half a barley seed of silver. The silver penny had considerable value in ancient times because fruit and vegetables were extremely reasonable and one penny could purchase a considerable amount. This is why a penny could be used to make the marriage valid. See Eisenstadt, op. cit., p. 609.

29. *Hagah, Orach Chaim* 694:1. See *Magen Avraham,* loc. cit., as well as *B'air Haitev, Shaarai T'shuvah,* and *Machtzith Ha'Shekel.* The practice is to donate a dollar and a half, or three times the half-shekel, because the word *terumah,* "offering," appears three times in the text, Exodus 30:11–16. Rabbi Barukh Halevi Epstein, *Torah Temimah,* Exodus 30:24, states that everyone in the synagogue—men, women, and children—should contribute this amount because all Jews were included in the miracle of Purim.

30. *Encyclopaedia Judaica,* vol. 16, col. 1095.

CHAPTER 18

1. *Yad, Issurai Bi'ah* 20:1–2; *Magen Avraham, Orach Chaim* 457:9; cf. Ezra 2:62–63. The terms *Cohen* and *Levi* are at times used interchangeably. Rabbi Joshua the son of Levi explained, "In twenty-four places *Cohanim* are called Levites and this is one of the instances: 'But the *Cohanim* the Levites the sons of Zadok" (*Bekhoroth* 4a; Ezekiel 44:15). We see that the *Cohanim* are described as Levites. Similarly, where the term "Levites" is used by itself, it also includes the priests. The Redemption of the First-Born, however, may only be conducted with a *Cohen,* not a *Levi.* See *Bekhoroth* 51; *Yoreh Deah* 305:3; *Pitchai T'shuvah* 5.

2. *Arukh HaShulchan* 305:12.

3. Rabbi Yaakov of Emden, *Beth Yaakov,* p. 104, par. 27; *Kitzur Shulchan Arukh* 164:6.

4. *Chullin* 130b based on 2 Chronicles 31:4. *Challah* 4:9, however, states that the redemption may be given to any *Cohen.*

5. Rabbi Yaakov of Emden, *Beth Yaakov,* p. 104.

6. *Challah* 4:9.

7. *Zokher HaBrith,* pp. 179 f.

8. *Chatham Sofer, Yoreh Deah* 301; Tosafoth, *Pesachim* 49b, s.v. *Amar.* However, *Chullin* 132a infers from Leviticus 6:13 and 7:33 that the duties and privileges designated for the sons of Aaron exclude the daughters of Aaron, since it is written, "Among the sons of Aaron."

9. *Bekhoroth* 49b.

10. *Zokher HaBrith,* p. 185, no. 10. *Chatham Sofer, Yoreh Deah* 134 says that it is permissible, since paper money is not a note of indebtedness. A note of indebtedness is not valid for redemption, in accordance with *Bekhoroth* 51a.

11. *Shakh* and *Taz, Yoreh Deah* 305:5.

12. *Berakhoth* 51b. See Tosafoth, loc. cit., s.v. *Hilkakh,* and *Rosh,* loc. cit.; *Yoreh Deah* 305:8 and *Taz* 305:6.

13. *Arukh HaShulchan* 305:27 and *Zokher HaBrith,* p. 186, no. 4.

14. Rabbi Abraham H. Noe, *Shiurai Torah* 3:43, fn. 100.

15. *Zokher HaBrith,* p. 182, nos. 8 and 9.

16. See Chapter 19.

CHAPTER 19

1. Exodus 13:12. See Rashi and *Mekhilta,* loc. cit.

2. *Arukh HaShulchan* 305:37.

3. *Aiduth L'Israel,* p. 179.

4. Ibid., p. 165, citing *Sefer HaEshkol,* vol. 2, no. 41 (Albak edition).

5. *Hagah, Yoreh Deah* 305:10.

6. *Yam Shel Shlomo* on *Kiddushin* 54.

7. *Baba Kama* 80a and Rashi, loc. cit., s.v. *Yeshua Haben.* Tosafoth, *Moed Katan* 8b, s.v. *Mipnai; Chakhmath Adam* 150:7.

8. *Zokher HaBrith,* p. 190, nos. 1, 2, based on *Hagah, Yoreh Deah* 305:10. See Chapter 21 for the service of the redemption.

9. *Sefer HaChinukh,* edited by Rabbi Chavel, p. 492; Rabbi Yaakov of Emden, *Beth Yaakov,* p. 105.

10. *Rosh,* end of *Bekhoroth,* and *Divrai Chamudoth,* loc. cit., 5.

11. *Yoreh Deah* 305:8 and *Shakh* 9.

12. *Pesachim* 121b; Tosafoth, *Sukkah* 46a, s.v. *Haoseh; Yad, Bekhorim* 11:5; *Yoreh Deah* 305:10; *Aiduth L'Yisrael,* p. 182.

13. *Zokher HaBrith,* p. 189, no. 15.

14. *Orach Chaim* 551:17.

15. *Sefer HaChinukh,* p. 492.

16. *Kitzur Shulchan Arukh* 164:4. *Aiduth L'Yisrael,* p. 171, states that this is the decision of Rav Hai Gaon.

17. *Aiduth L'Yisrael,* p. 171.

18. *T'rumath HaDeshen* 268; *Hagah, Yoreh Deah* 305:10; *Zokher HaBrith*, p. 188.

19. *Sefer HaChinukh*, p. 492, refers to this blessing. It is not a generally accepted custom.

20. *Aiduth L'Yisrael*, p. 178.

21. J.D. Eisenstein, *Otzar Dinim U'Minhagim*, p. 333.

22. *Aiduth L'Yisrael*, p. 167.

23. See Chapter 21.

24. See Chapter 21.

CHAPTER 20

1. Exodus 13:1–2.

2. Exodus 13:13.

3. Exodus 22:28.

4. Exodus 34:20.

5. Numbers 3:11–13.

6. Numbers 3:40–50.

7. Numbers 8:16–18.

8. Numbers 18:16.

9. *Bekhoroth* 4a, citing Ezekiel 44:15.

10. *Sanhedrin* 17a, based on Numbers 3:47; *Numbers Rabbah*, loc. cit.; *Tanchuma* 3:16–18; *Yalkut Shimoni* 693.

11. *Zevachim* 112b, based on Exodus 24:5. See also *Bekhoroth* 4b.

12. *Bekhoroth* 4b and 5a. *Yalkut Shimoni* 364 cites the *Sifri* that whenever the word *li* appears, as in *ki li kol bekhor* (Numbers 8:17), this signifies an eternal relationship. *Emek Davar* on Exodus 3:13 maintains that the first-born has a special holiness to this day.

13. *Kiddushin* 29a.

14. *Kiddushin* 30b.

15. *Sforno* on Numbers 8:18.

16. *Yad, Bekhorim* 1:10. Rashi in *Kiddushin* 8a and *Chullin* 132a, s.v. *Rav Kahana*, maintains that the husband of a *Coheneth*, the daughter of a *Cohen*, can accept the redemption for his wife. Tosafoth and Rosh, loc. cit., state that in this instance there were two rabbis with the same name, one of whom was a *Cohen*.

17. Rashi, Numbers 3:12; *Numbers Rabbah* 3:45.

18. Rashi, Numbers 3:46.

19. *Sheeltoth*, Exodus 46 on Exodus 13:2.

20. Maimonides, *Sefer HaMitzvoth*, Positive Commandment 79.

21. *Mekhilta* 18:124.

22. *Yalkut Shimoni,* Numbers 8, quoting the *Tanchuma.*
23. Abarbanel on Exodus 13. See Isaiah 49:14.
24. Malbim on Exodus 11:5. See Ezekiel 20:31, 2 Kings 3:27, and Micah 6:7.
25. *Exodus Rabbah* 19, end of *Bo.*
26. *Minchath Chinukh,* p. 64.
27. Hirsch, *Pentateuch,* p. 162.
28. *Chatham Sofer, Yoreh Deah* 234.

CHAPTER 21

1. Before commencing the redemption rite, the *Cohen* ascertains from the mother that this child is actually her first-born. It is possible that she had previously had a miscarriage of a fetus that was forty days or older, and then she would not be obligated to redeem her son.

When wine is not available, the washing of the hands and the blessing over the bread take place after the redemption. This meal is a festive meal (*Seudath Mitzvah*). See Rashi, *Baba Kama* 80a, s.v. *Yeshua*; Tosafoth, *Moed Katan* 8b, s.v. *Mipnai*; *Hagah, Orach Chaim* 551:9; *Mishnah B'rurah* 232:24.

2. This is the accepted text. The verses are from Numbers 18:16 and Exodus 13:2.

3. The Aramaic language is used because it dates from the time of the Gaonim, who resided in Babylonia, and it was the language best understood by the populace. Rav Hai Gaon maintains that Hebrew may be used instead. See *T'shuvath HaGaonim, Shaarai T'shuvah* 47. The Hebrew text is found in *Siddur Avodath Yisrael* (Rödelheim, 1956), p. 584: מַה אַתָּה חָפֵץ יוֹתֵר בְּנְךָ בְּכוֹרְךָ אוֹ חָמֵשׁ סְלָעִים שֶׁאַתָּה חַיָּיב בְּפִדְיוֹנוּ?

The *Cohen's* question appears to give the father the option of redeeming or not redeeming his son. *Aiduth L'Yisrael,* p. 179, explains that in reality there is no choice. The father cannot give the child to the *Cohen* and is obliged to redeem him, since this is a Biblical commandment. The question is asked to make the *mitzvah* more desirable to the father, so that he will redeem his child of his own free will.

4. The response of the father is taken from the Rosh, *Kiddushin* 1:41. This response, too, may be said in Hebrew: בְּנִי בְכוֹרִי אֲנִי חָפֵץ, וְהֵילָךְ חָמֵשׁ סְלָעִים לְפִדְיוֹנוּ.

5. *Pesachim* 121b.

6. Ibid. This blessing may be said even when the father is in mourning; so *Orach Chaim* 551:17, *Magen Avraham,* loc. cit., s.k. 42, and *Aiduth L'Yisrael,* p. 182.

7. *Sefer HaChinukh, mitzvah* 389.

8. Genesis 48:20.

9. Numbers 6:24–26.

10. Psalm 121:5.

11. Proverbs 3:2, Psalm 121:7. *Aiduth L'Yisrael,* p. 202, offers an additional prayer that was said by the *Cohen.* This prayer is based on the teachings of Rabbi Israel Isserlein, which were compiled by Rabbi Joseph ben Moses (1423–1490) in *Leket Yosher* (ed. by J. Freimann, 1903). *Sefer HaChinukh, mitzvah* 389, presents the same prayer. Rabbi Yaakov of Emden, *Beth Yaakov,* permits the saying of this prayer. The following is the text:

ברוך אתה יי אלהינו מלך העולם, אשר קידש עובר במעי אמו, ולארבעים יום חלק אבריו, רמ"ח אברים. ואחר כך נפח בו נשמה, ככתוב ויפח באפיו נשמת רוח חיים, עור ובשר הלבישו ובעצמות וגידים סככו. ככתוב עור ובשר תלבישני ובעצמות וגידים תסוככני. וצוה לו מאכל ומשתה, דבש וחלב להתענג בו, וזימן לו שני מלאכי השרת לשמרו בתוך מעי אמו, ככתוב: חיים וחסד עשית עמדי. (אמו אומרת) זה בני בכורי שבו פתח הקב"ה דלתי בטני. (אביו אומר) זה בני בכורי הוא, ואני מוזהר לפדותו, שנאמר וכל בכור אדם בבניך תפדה. יהי רצון מלפניך יי אלהי, שכשם שזכית את אביו לפדותו, כן תזכהו לתורה ולחופה ולמעשים טובים. ברוך אתה יי מקדש בכורי ישראל לפדיונם.

12. This text is from Rabbi Yaakov of Emden, *Beth Yaakov,* p. 105. See *Kiddushin* 29a and *Yoreh Deah* 305:15.

13. See note 5.

14. See note 6.

15. See note 7.

16. See note 8.

17. See note 9.

18. See note 10.

19. See note 11.

20. This text is found in *Aiduth L'Yisrael,* p. 189, and it is taken from *Likutai Pinchas,* who brings it from *Machaneh Chaim* 3:75.

21. See note 2.

22. See note 5.

23. See note 6.

24. See note 7.

25. See note 8.

26. See note 9.

27. See note 10.

28. See note 11.

29. The text is from *Siddur HaShalaim* (Jerusalem: Eshkol, n.d.), p. 132.

30. See note 3.

31. See note 4.

32. See note 5.

33. See note 6.

34. This text is from *Aiduth L'Yisrael,* p. 194.

35. Rabbi David de Sola Pool, ed. and trans., *Book of Prayer* (New York: Union of Sephardic Cngregations, 1941, 1960), p. 418.

36. See note 2.

37. See note 5.

38. See note 6.

39. The priestly blessing does not have the formality of the Ashkenazic rite but contains its substance. Note that the blessing on wine is also omitted.

APPENDIX 1

1. For a detailed presentation of the gross anatomy as well as very helpful illustrations, see Carmine Clemente, *Anatomy: A Regional Atlas of the Human Body* (Philadelphia: Lea & Fabiger, 1978), Figs. 239-244, or *Gray's Anatomy,* edited by Roger Warwick and Peter L. Williams, 35th British ed. (Philadelphia: W.B. Saunders Co., 1973), pp. 1345-1348.

2. See Chapter 4.

APPENDIX 2

1. *Symposium on Medical Dilemmas and the Practise of Milah,* p. 9.

2. Information regarding the Anprolene Gas Sterilizing Kit may be obtained from H.W. Andersen Products, Inc., 45 East Main Street, Oyster Bay, N.Y. 11771. Sterilizer bags and gas sensitive tapes are available at Bard Sterilizing System, Vendor: General Medical, Murray Hill, N.J.

3. Rav Hai Gaon in *Responsa Shaarai Tzedek,* (Salonika, 801), s. 6 states: "The *mohel* cuts both the prepuce and the membrane at the same time." So too, Rabbi Ishmael HaCohen, *Responsa Zera Emeth* 3:132. Rabbi Moshe Feinstein, *Iggroth Moshe,* p. 135, states: "It is obvious that it makes no difference how the glans is made visible."

4. Rabbi Yaakov Emden, in his *Siddur, Beth Yaakov,* p. 101, s. 61, recommends the use of the probe. A set of *mohel*'s instruments dating from 1801 includes a probe.

5. Rabbi Ephraim Rubin, in a lecture on technique at the Brith Milah School Conducted at The Mount Sinai Hospital.

6. *Shabbath* 133a.

7. This decision is recorded in *Yad Eliezer* by Rabbi Eliezer Horowitz, s. 55.

Authorities agreeing with the *Chatham Sofer* include Rabbi Samson R. Hirsch, Rabbi Isaac Elchanan Spector, and Rabbi Yechiel Epstein. See *Sefer HaBris*, p. 216 and *Dam Brith*, p. 43.

8. Rabbi Moshe D. Tendler in *Symposium*, p. 13.

9. Rabbi Yoseph E. Henkin wrote in *Aiduth L'Yisrael*, published by the Union of Orthodox Rabbis, p. 144, that when the infant's father insists that the *mohel* use this instrument, it is permissible for him to do so. See also *Hapardes* 18 (Menachem Av 5704 [1944]:8.

10. Chief Rabbi Isaac Halevy Herzog issued a proclamation on 28 Teveth 5716 (1956) that the Magen Clamp is perfectly permissible. In this proclamation he wrote that he agrees with Rabbi Eliezer Silver, president of the Union of Orthodox Rabbis. Rabbi Moshe D. Tendler wrote in *Halachah Bulletin*, published for the Medical-Dental Section of the Association of Orthodox Jewish Scientists, that "the Magen clamp should not be used to perform ritual circumcision." He explained his reasoning: "(1) If the clamp is left on for an extended period of time (more than a few minutes), complete hemostasis will result so that no free blood occurs; and (2) the use of clamps might lead to circumcision becoming a surgical rather than a ritual procedure."

APPENDIX 3

1. Milton Malev, "The Jewish Orthodox Circumcision Ceremony," *Journal American Psychoanalytic Association,* July 1966, pp. 510–517; Harry Apfel, M.D., "Ritual Circumcision," *Archives of Pediatrics* 68 (1951): 427–430; Harold Speert, M.D., "Circumcision of the Newborn," *Obstetrics and Gynecology* 2, no. 2 (August 1953): 164–172; Abraham Ravich, M.D., "Viral Carcinogenesis in Venereally Susceptible Organs," *Cancer* 27, no. 6 (June 1971): 1493–1496; Elizabeth Stern, M.D., and Peter A. Lachenbruch, M.D., "Circumcision Information in a Cancer Detection Center Population," *Journal of Chronic Diseases* 21 (1968): 117–124; Gocke Cansever, "Psychological Effects of Circumcision," *British Journal of Medical Psychology* 38, no. 4 (1965): 321–331; Daniel Whiddon, M.D., "The Widdicombe File," *Lancet,* August 15, 1953, pp. 337–338; Charles Weiss, M.D., "Ritual Circumcision," *Clinical Pediatrics,* October 1962, pp. 65–72; Frank Hinman, M.D., review of *Circumcision: An American Health Fallacy* by Edward Wallerstein, *Journal of the American Medical Association,* 304, no. 10 (1981): 619; Robert P. Bolande, M.D.,"Ritualistic Surgery—Circumcision and Tonsillectomy," *New England Journal of Medicine* 280, no. 11 (March 13, 1969): 591–596; D. St. John-Hunt, "Correspondence," *New England Journal of Medicine* 281, no. 11 (March 13, 1969): 621–622; William K. C. Morgan, M.D., "The Rape of the Phallus," *Journal of the American Medical Association* 193, no.

3 (July 19, 1965): 223–224; Editorial, "The Case Against Neonatal Circumcision," *British Medical Journal,* May 5, 1979, pp. 1163–1164; Elliot Leiter, M.D., and Albert M. Lefkovits, M.D., "Circumcision and Penile Carcinoma," *New York State Journal of Medicine,* August 1975, pp. 1520–1522; Zdenek S. Prucha, M.D. (no title), *CMA Journal* 122 (April 5, 1980): 834; Anon., "Circumcision: A Balanced Report Based on Facts, Not Conjecture," *Patient Care,* July 15, 1971, pp. 56–86; Fred Rosner, M.D., "Circumcision—Attempt at Clearer Understanding," *New York State Journal of Medicine,* November 15, 1966, pp. 2919–2922; E. Noel Preston, "Whither the Foreskin," *Journal of the American Medical Association,* 213, no. 11 (September 14, 1970): 1853–1858; Leonard J. Marino, M.D., "Counterpoint," *Nassau County Medical Center Proceedings,* Autumn 1980, pp. 103–106; Charles Schlosberg, M.D., "Thirty Years of Ritual Circumcisions," *Clinical Pediatrics* 10, no. 4 (April 1971): 205–209; Howard H. Schlossman, M.D., "Circumcision as Defense," *Psychoanalytic Quarterly* 5, no. 3 (July 1966): 340–356; Robert Burger, M.D., and Thomas H. Guthrie, M.D., "Why Circumcision?" *Pediatrics* 54, no. 3 (September 1974); Hugh C. Thompson, M.D., et al., "Report of the Ad Hoc Task Force on Circumcision," *Pediatrics* 56, no. 4, (October 1975): 610; John L. Wirth, M.D., "Statistics on Circumcision in Canada and Australia," *American Journal of Obstetrics and Gynecology* 130 (1978): 236; Elliot Grossman, M.D., and Norman Ames Posner, M.D., "Surgical Circumcision of Neonates: A History of Its Development," *Obstetrics and Gynecology* 58 (1981): 241; Gerhart S. Schwartz, M.D., review of *Circumcision: An American Health Fallacy* in *Bulletin of the New York Academy of Medicine* 57, no. 9 (November 1981): 817–821; Jacob Oster, M.D., "Further Fate of the Foreskin," *Archives of the Diseases of Childhood,* 43 (1968): 200–203; Anon., "Routine Circumcision Is Sharply Condemned," *Pediatrics Herald,* November 1965; Hawa Patel, M.B., "The Problem of Routine Circumcision," *Canadian Medical Association Journal* 95 (September 10, 1966): 576–581. Mosze Kochen, M.D., and Stephen McCurdy, M.P.H., "Circumcision and the Risk of Cancer of the Penis," *American Journal of the Diseases of Children,* 134 (May 1980): 484–486; O.G. Dodge et al., "Circumcision and the Incidence of Carcinoma of the Penis and Cervix," *East African Medical Journal* 40 (September 1963): 440–442; Richard L. Miller, M.S., and Donald C. Snyder, M.D., "Immediate Circumcision of the Newborn Male," *American Journal of Obstetrics and Gynecology* 65 (January 1953): 1–11; Syndey S. Gellis, M.D., "Circumcision," *American Journal of Diseases of Children* 132 (1978): 1168–1169; Abraham Steinberg, M.D., ed., *Assia,* no. 29/30 (June 1981): 21–42.

2. Jane E. Brody, "A Restudy Urged on Circumcision," *New York Times,* September 21, 1970; Jane E. Brody, "Personal Health," *New York Times,* January 24, 1979; Mark Liff, "The Kindest Cut," *Daily News,* January 25, 1981, pp. 16–20; Adon Taft, "Attacks on Circumcision Branded Anti-Semitic by Some Noted Rabbis," *Miami Herald,* March 27, 1981, p. 5C; Jay H. Leve, "Tradition

Lives," *Miami Herald,* April 9, 1981, p. 1B; Jennifer Bolch, "Circumcision: Is Old Rite Wrong?" Syndicated article by *Dallas Times Herald,* published in *New Jersey Record,* September 14, 1981, p. B5; Linda Matchan, "The Question of Circumcision," *Boston Globe,* February 15, 1982, p. 21.

3. John M. Foley, M.D., "The Unkindest Cut of All," *Fact Magazine,* July–August 1966, pp. 3–9; Erich Isaac, "The Enigma of Circumcision," *Commentary,* January 1967, pp. 51–55; "The Medical Controversy Over Circumcision," *Good Housekeeping,* September 1968, p. 179; "Cancer," *Time,* November 14, 1969, p. 77; "Rating the Circumcisers," *Newsweek,* September 4, 1972, p. 67; Karen E. Paige, "The Ritual of Circumcision," *Human Nature,* May 1978, pp. 40–48; Steven Levy, "The First Rite of Man," *Esquire,* May 1981, pp. 96–99; John Langone, "The Unkindest Cut," *Discover,* July 1981, pp. 74–75; "A Son's Rite," *Time,* August 31, 1981, p. 57; Gideon C. Panter, "Circumcision: Making the Choice," *Parents,* July 1981, p. 82; Carl Otten, M.D., "The Case Against Newborn Circumcision," *Saturday Evening Post,* December 1981, pp. 30 ff.; Cory SerVaas, M.D., "Health Groups Conclude: 'Routine Circumcision Not Recommended,'" *Saturday Evening Post,* December 1981, pp. 26 ff.

4. Charles Weiss, "A Worldwide Survey of the Current Practice of Milah (Ritual Circumcision)," *Jewish Social Studies,* January 1962, pp. 30–48; Moshe Halevi Spero and Julian Gordon, M.D., "Postponement of Ritual Circumcision in Young Children for Psychiatric Reasons—A Halakhic Analysis," *Intercom* 19, no. 1 (February 1980): 23–31. This article deals with the circumcision of Russian-Jewish children where such problems may occur. It does not refer to the eight-day-old child.

5. Abraham Ravich, M.D., *Preventing V.D. and Cancer by Circumcision* (New York: Philosophical Library, 1973); Edward Wallerstein, *Circumcision: An American Health Fallacy* (New York: Springer Publications, 1980).

6. "NBC Magazine," produced by the National Broadcasting Company. This show appeared on national television on October 2, 1981. "Today Show" NBC Network, December 29, 1981.

7. February 11, 1979.

8. Arthur I. Eidelman, M.D., defined the phrase "No absolute medical indications," in a personal communication to this writer. He wrote, "Despite the distortions related in the lay press, the Academy does not condemn circumcision but rather recommends the nonsurgical alternatives for proper care of the genitalia.

9. Dr. Leiter is referring to the eighth day.

10. See note 8.

11. A letter from Dr. Leiter to this writer, dated December 10, 1981.

Bibliography

Many of the books in this bibliography are listed by title or acronym rather than by the author's name. When it is assumed that the reader is familiar with the author's name, the name of the author appears first. An alphabetical rather than chronological listing is followed to facilitate locating the text.

Since this bibliography includes literature from many periods, it would be best to begin with an outline of the development of *Halakhah,* so that the reader may have a clearer picture.

The basis of Jewish law is the Torah, which was dictated to Moses by God (1272 B.C.E.). The Prophets and the Writings appeared subsequently. These three sets of books were accepted in the Canon (ca. 2d cent. C.E.) and comprise the Bible, or the Written Law.

We depend on the Oral Law to comprehend the Written Law. It is called the Oral Law because it is a body of information that was transmitted orally from generation to generation. Rabbi Yehudah Hanasi, realizing that the Oral Law might be forgotten, recorded the tradition in the Mishnah (188 C.E.). A parallel work is the *Baraitha,* or rabbinic statements that were not included in the Mishnah. The Midrash began appearing at approximately the same time as the Mishnah and the *Baraitha.* This work interprets the Bible on a devotional level as it searches for the Bible's inner meaning.

The Mishnah was studied and expounded over a period of centuries, and these interpretations were committed to writing in the Talmud. One Talmud was published in Jerusalem and is called the *Yerushalmi* or the Jerusalem Talmud (ca. 230 C.E.). The second was developed in Babylonia and is known as the *Bavli* or the Babylonian Talmud (505 C.E.).

The latter works were blessed with numerous commentaries

169

which were written during several eras. The Gaonim, leaders of the Academies in Babylonia, were the first, writing from 600 to 1038 C.E. They were followed by the Rishonim, or "first [codifiers]" (1038–1572). The period of the Rishonim ended when the Shulchan Arukh, the Code of Jewish Law, was published and we entered into the period of the Acharonim, or "later [codifiers]."

Another body of literature—the Responsa—was fashioned to serve a specific need. The Talmud and the *Shulchan Arukh* do not cover every situation. Consequently, rabbis would often seek guidance on specific questions from the leading authorities. The Responsa literature records the questions and responses. This format began during the time that the Talmud was evolving and continues to this day. There are approximately 3,000 volumes of Responsa literature in print and in manuscript form. Consult Rabbi Aryeh Kaplan's *The Handbook of Jewish Thought,* pp. 59–286, for additional information.

BIBLE: COMMENTARIES AND TRANSLATIONS

Abarbanel. Rabbi Isaac ben Judah Abrabanel (1437–1508). First published in Venice, 1579. The Jerusalem edition, published 1964, was used for this book.

Adereth Eliahu. Rabbi Eliahu ben Shlomoh Zalman (1720–1797), better known as the Gaon of Vilna.

Akaidath Yitzchak. Rabbi Yitzchak Arama (1420–1494). First published in Salonika, 1522.

Aquila (ca. 120 C.E.). Author of a Greek translation of the Torah.

Bible (Tanakh). Jerusalem: Eshkol, no date.

Chizkuni. Rabbi Chezkiah ben Manoach (ca. 1250). First published in Cremona, 1559.

Deuteronomy Rabbah. See *Midrash Rabbah.*

Ha'amek Davar. Rabbi Naphtali Z. Berlin. Jerusalem, 1958.

Exodus Rabbah. See *Midrash Rabbah.*

Genesis Rabbah. See *Midrash Rabbah.*

Ibn Ezra. Rabbi Avraham ben Meir (1089–1164). First published in Naples, 1488, this commentary is included in the *Mikra'oth G'doloth.*

Jonathan ben Uzziel. (1st cent. B.C.E.) Aramaic translation, appears in the *Mikra'oth G'doloth.*

JPS. Translation of the Bible into English by the Jewish Publication Society of America, Philadelphia, 1917.

K'li Yakar. Rabbi Shlomo Ephraim ben Aaron (1550–1619). Published in Lublin, 1602; included in the *Mikra'oth G'doloth.*

Leviticus Rabbah. See *Midrash Rabbah.*

Living Torah, The. Rabbi Aryeh Kaplan. New York: Maznaim Publishing Corp., 1981.

Mai'am Lo'aiz. See *Torah Anthology.*

Malbim. Acronym for Rabbi Meir Leib ben Yechiel Michael (Weiser) (1809–1879), the author of *HaTorah V'Ha'Mitzvoth,* first published in Warsaw, 1860–76.

Metzudath David and *Metzudath Tzion.* David and Jehiel Hillel Altschuler. First published in Leghorn, 1780–82. These commentaries appear in many editions of the Hebrew Bible.

Midrash Rabbah. Important collection of Midrashic teachings from the Gaonic era. Published many times; English translation: Soncino, London, 1939.

Mikra'oth G'doloth. Edited by Joel Levenson and Menachem Mendel Mendelson. Includes thirty-two commentaries; published in Warsaw, 1860.

Numbers Rabbah. See *Midrash Rabbah.*

Pentateuch, The. Translation and commentary by Rabbi Samson R. Hirsch. Rendered into English by Isaac Levy. 2d ed., New York: Judaica Press, 1971.

Perush HaRamban al HaTorah. Nachmanides (Moshe ben Nachman) (1194–1270). Critical edition edited by Rabbi Charles B. Chavel. Jerusalem: Mossad Harav Kook, 1972.

Pesikta D'Rav Kahana. One of the oldest *Midrashim.*

Pirkai Rabbi Eliezer. Midrash attributed to Rabbi Eliezer ben Hyrcanus. First published in Constantinople, 1514; republished many times.

Radak. Acronym for Rabbi David Kimchi (1160?–1235?). First published in Pressburg, 1842.

Ralbag. Acronym for Rabbi Levi ben Gershom (1288–1344). First published in Mantua, 1475.

Rashi. Acronym for Rabbi Solomon ben Isaac of Troyes (1040–1105). His commentary on the Bible and Talmud has been reprinted many times.

Scroll of the Hasmoneans, The Megilath Chanukah is published in *Avodat Israel,* edited by Hyman Charlop (New York: Hebrew Publishing Co., 1931).

Sekhel Tov. Rabbi Menachem ben Shlomo (ca. 1120). Midrashic work edited by Shlomo Buber, Berlin, 1900.

Sforno. Rabbi Obadiah ben Jacob Sforno (ca. 1470–1550). This commentary first appeared in Venice, 1567.

Shadal. Acronym for Rabbi Samuel David Luzzatto (1800–1865).

Sif'thai Chakhamim. Shabbatai Bass (1641–1718). First published in Frankfurt a.M., 1712. Commentary on Rashi, appearing side by side with Rashi's work.

Sifra. Attributed to Rav (ca. 220 C.E.). Midrash on Leviticus. First published in Bucharest, 1523; critically edited by A.H. Weiss, Vienna, 1862.

Sifri. Attributed to Rav (ca. 220 C.E.). Midrash on the books of Numbers and Deuteronomy. Critical edition by H.S. Horowitz and A.A. Finkelstein, Berlin, 1934–39.

Tanchuma. Midrash on the Torah attributed to Rabbi Tanchuma bar Abba (ca. 370 C.E.). Printed first time in Constantinople, 1522. Critical edition by Shlomo Buber, Jerusalem: Eshkol, 1972.

Targum Onkeles. Translation of the Bible into Aramaic (ca. 90 C.E.); appears in many editions of the Bible.

Targum Yonathan. Yonathan ben Uziel (1st cent. C.E.). Aramaic translation.

Tol'doth Yitzchak. Rabbi Yitzchak Caro (1458–1535). First printed in Constantinople, 1518. The author of this work was the uncle of Rabbi Yosef Caro.

Torah Anthology, The. This work is by Rabbi Yaakov Culi (1689–1732) and was written in Ladino. It is currently being translated into English by Rabbi Aryeh Kaplan. The first volume was published in New York by Maznaim Press, 1977. Ten volumes have appeared to date.

Torah Sh'laimah. Anthology of Midrashim and early commentaries on the Torah compiled by Rabbi Menachem S. Kasher (b. 1895). First volume published in Jerusalem, 1926, with over thirty subsequent volumes.

Torah Temimah. Rabbi Barukh Halevi Epstein (1860–1942). First published in Vilna, 1904; republished in Tel Aviv, 1942.

Yalkut Shimoni. Rabbi Shimon Ashkenazi (ca. 1260). First published in Leghorn, 1650; reprinted in New York and Berlin, 1925.

Yismach Moshe. Rabbi Moshe Teitelbaum (1759–1841). First published in Sighet, 1906; republished in New York, 1977.

Zohar. Attributed to Rabbi Simeon ben Yochai. First published at the beginning of the fourteenth century; republished many times.

RABBINIC WORKS (HEBREW)

Abudarham. David ben Joseph Abudarham (14th cent.). Jerusalem, 1962, pp. 350–357.

Aiduth L'Yisrael. Article by Rabbi Y. E. Henkin. Edited by Oscar Z. Rand. New York, no date.

Aiduth L'Yisrael. Jacob Werdiger. Tel Aviv, 1976.

Arugath HaBosem. Liturgical commentary by Rabbi Avraham ben Azriel (ca. 1230). Edited by Rabbi Ephraim Orbach. Jerusalem, 1947.

Atereth Paz. Sheftel Davidson. Tel Aviv, 1944/45.

Atereth Z'kainim. Rabbi Menachem M. Auerback. In *Orach Chaim.* See *Shulchan Arukh.*

Avodah Zarah. Talmudic tractate dealing with prohibition against idolatry.

Avoth D'Rabbi Nathan. Critical edition by Professor Solomon Schechter. Reprinted in New York, 1945.

Ba'alai Ha'Nefesh. Rabbi Abraham ben David of Posquières, known as Rabad (1125–1198). Berlin, 1762.

Baba Bathra. Talmudic tractate dealing with claims to do or possess something, or to prevent another person from possessing or doing something.

Baba Kama. Talmudic tractate dealing with rabbinic views regarding civil law.

Bach. Hagaoth Bayith Chadash or *Hagaoth HaBach.* Rabbi Joel Sirkes (1561–1640). In Romm edition of Talmud. See below, "Responsa Literature."

B'air Haitev. Rabbi Zechariah Mendel ben Aryeh Leib (d. after 1707). In Romm edition of *Shulchan Arukh.*

B'air Yaakov. Jacob Glassberg. Commentary on *Zikhron Brith L'Rishonim.* Cracow, 1852.

Bavli. Babylonian Talmud. See *Talmud.*

Bekhoroth. Talmudic tractate concerned with first-born.

Berakhoth. Talmudic tractate dealing with correct time to say prayers.

Bertinoro. Rabbi Obadiah Bertinoro (1450–1516). Commentary included in many editions of the Mishnah.

Bikkurim. Talmudic tractate discussing offering of first fruits.

Biur HaGra. Rabbi Eliyahu ben Shlomoh Zalman (Gaon of Vilna) (1720–1797). In Romm edition of *Shulchan Arukh.*

Brith Avoth, Hilkhoth Milah. Rabbi Shabbathai Lipschitz. First printed in Munkács, 1904; republished in New York, 1969.

Brith Avraham, Dinai Milah. Zvi B. Auerbach. Frankfurt, 1880; Jerusalem, 1907.

Brith Avraham, Ha'Ma'aseh Limlekheth HaMilah. Samuel Dov Igelberg. Warsaw, 1888.

Brith David. Avraham Reich. Jerusalem, 1981.

Brith Olam. Dawid Rundo. Warsaw, 1883.

Brith Olam. Jacob H. Bloom. New York, 1949.

Brith Shalom. Rabbi Nachmon and Rabbi Nathan of Bratslav. Brooklyn, 1979.

Brith Shalom. Menahem Sherhei. Vilna, 1906; section 2:3.

Brith Shalom. Shalom Wachman. Warsaw, 1928–29.

Brith Yitzchok ben Avraham. Isaac Bukatman. Vilna, 1906.

Brith Zion. Ben Zion Alfas. Vilna, 1924. Work discussing *Brith Milah, Pidyon Haben,* and education of children.

Chagigah. Talmudic tractate whose title signifies "festal offering."

Chakhmath Adam. Rabbi Abraham Danzig (1748–1820). Stettin, 1863.

Challah. Talmudic tractate dealing with laws of dough (*challah*) to be given to *Cohanim.*

Chananel, Rabainu (d. ca. 1056). Commentary included in Romm edition of Talmud.

Choshen Mishpat. See *Shulchan Arukh.*

Chothem Kodesh. Jacob Levine. Cracow, 1891. Work presenting laws of *Brith Milah.*

Chukath Hagair. Rabbi Moshe Steinberg. Jerusalem, 1971.

Chullin. Talmudic tractate discussing dietary laws.

Dam Brith, Metzitzah B'kli. Alexander Tertis, London, 1900.

Darkhai Moshe. Rabbi Moses ben Israel Isserles (1520–1572). Sulzbach, 1652.

Divrai Chamudoth. Commentary on the Rosh by Rabbi Yom Tov Lipmann Heller (1579–1654). In Romm edition of Talmud.

Eruvin. Talmudic tractate devoted to the fusion of a private and a public domain to satisfy the laws of the Sabbath.

Gittin. Talmudic tractate concerned primarily with the document known as *Get,* the legal instrument in divorce.

Hagah. Also known as *Ramah* and *Mappah.* Work offering observances of Ashkenazic Jews by Rabbi Moses ben Israel Isserles (see *Darkhai Moshe*); included in *Shulchan Arukh.*

Haga'oth Smak. Commentary on *Sepher Mitzvoth Katan* by Rabbi Peretz ben Eliyahu: see *Smak.* Satmar, 1934.

Hai Gaon (939–1038). Commentary on Mishnah in Romm edition of Talmud.

HaGra. See *Biur HaGra.*

Hilkhoth Rav Alfas. Rabbi Isaac ben Jacob Alfasi (1013–1103). The Vienna edition, 1835, is used here.

Ikrai Dinim. Rabbi Doniel Tierni. In Romm edition of *Yoreh Deah.*

Imrai Yosher. Rabbi Meier Arak. Munkàcs, 1854, 1925. Section 1.

Keritoth. Talmudic tractate dealing with offense for which punishment is *kareth* (divine "cutting off").

Kethuboth. Talmudic tractate defining rights and duties of husband and wife.

Kad HaKemach. Rabbi Bachya ben Asher (d. 1340). Translated and annotated by Rabbi Charles B. Chavel. Shilo Press, 1980.

Koraith HaBrith. Rabbi Elia Poisek. Lvov, 1892.

Kiddushin. Talmudic tractate dealing with betrothal and marriage.

Kitvai HaRamban. Nachmanides. Ed. and annotated by Rabbi Charles B. Chavel. Jerusalem: Mossad Harav Kook, 1963.

Kitzur Shulchan Arukh. Rabbi Solomon Ganzfried, Warsaw, 1864.

Kuntrath HaSfaikoth. Yehudah Heller. Munkàcs, 1850.

Kuntrath Metzitzah. Y. Margolies-Yaffe. Pressburg, 1899.

Leket Yosher. Compilation of Rabbi Israel Isserlein's works by Rabbi Joseph ben Moses (1423–1490?). Edited by J. Freimann. Berlin, 1903.

Likutai Pinchas. Pinchas Z. Schwartz. New York: Kol Aryeh Research Institute, 1973.

Machtzith HaShekel. Commentary on *Magen Avraham* by Rabbi Shmu'ail HaLevy of Cologne. In *Orach Chaim.*

Magen Avraham. Rabbi Abraham Abele ben Chaim Gombiner (1637–1683).

Maharsha. Rabbi Samuel Eliezer ben Judah haLevi Edels (1555–1631).

Mahrik. Rabbi Joseph ben Solomon Colon (1420–1480). Shoresh 143.

Maishiv Nefesh. Menahem Loeb Scherhey. Vilna, 1905.

Makhshirai Mila. Elijah Shamma. Leghorn, 1793.

Megillah. Talmudic tractate concerned primarily with Book of Esther.

Mekhilta. Earliest commentary on Book of Exodus, by school of Rabbi Yishmael (ca. 120 C.E.); first printed in Constantinople, 1515.

Menachoth. Talmudic tractate dealing mainly with regulations governing meal offerings brought to the Temple in Jerusalem.

Migdal Oz. Commentary to *Mishnah Torah* by Rabbi Shem Tov ben Abraham Ibn Gaon (14th cent.). In Vilna edition, 1900.

Migdal Oz. Rabbi Yaakov of Emden. Reprinted Jerusalem: Eshkol, 1974.

Minchath Cohen. Abraham Pimental (17th cent.). Amsterdam, 1668.

Minchath Shmu'ail. Critical and annotated edition of *Sheeltoth De Rav Ahai Gaon* by Rabbi Samuel K. Mirsky. Jerusalem: Sura Research and Publication Foundation, Yeshiva University, 1959–80.

Mishnah B'rurah. Rabbi Israel Meir Kahan (1838–1933). Warsaw, 1852–58; Jerusalem, 1977.

Mishnah Torah, Yad HaChazaka. Rambam, acronym for Rabbi Moses ben Maimon (1135–1204). Numerous editions.

Mitzvath HaMetzitzah. Sinai Schiffer. Jerusalem, 1965.

Moed Katan. Talmudic tractate devoted to regulations of mourning during intermediate days of Passover and Sukkoth.

Moreh Derekh L'Mohalim. M. Lenski, Warsaw, 1931.

Nachal HaBrith. Osher A. Katz. New York, 1973.

Nedarim. Talmudic tractate dealing with vows made to deny oneself permitted pleasures.

Niddah. Talmudic tractate dealing with restrictions on women during menstrual period.

Nishmath Chaim. Solomon Feinsilber. Jerusalem, 1907.

Orach Chaim. See *Shulchan Arukh.*

Oth Brith, Hilkhoth Milah U'Pidyon Haben. Simon Sidon (1815–1891). Pressburg, 1850.

Oth Chaim V'Shalom. Rabbi Elazar Schapiro. Munkàcs, 1919; Jerusalem, 1964.

Palestinian Talmud or *Yerushalmi.* See *Talmud.* Vilna: Romm, 1895.

Perush HaMishnayoth L'haRambam. See *Mishnah Torah.* Commentary on Mishnah; included in most editions of Babylonian Talmud.

Pesachim. Talmudic tractate dealing with laws of Passover.

Pidyon Nefesh. Work dealing with Redemption of First-Born by Rabbi Shabbatai Lifshitz. Munkàcs, 1901; reprinted 1968.

Pithchai T'shuva. Rabbi Abraham Zevi Hirsch Eisenstadt (1813–1868). In *Shulchan Arukh.*

Pri M'gadim. Rabbi Yosef Teomim (1727–1792). In *Shulchan Arukh.*

Rama. See *Hagah.*

Rosh Hashanah. Talmudic tractate dealing with two subjects—arranging calendar and service for New Year.

Sanhedrin. Talmudic tractate discussing higher courts of law.

S'dai Chemed. Rabbi Chaim Medini (1832–1904). Warsaw, 1891–1912. Vol. 6, pp. 343–374.

Sefer Chassidim. Rabbi Judah ben Samuel haChassid (d. 1217). Published 1832.

Sefer Darkhai Noam. Rabbi Mordecai ben Judah (d. 1684). Venice, 1697.

Sefer HaBris. Rabbi Moshe B. Pirutinsky. New York, 1972.

Sefer HaBrith. Benjamin Niederhofheim. Frankfurt, 1841.

Sefer HaBrith. Phineas Elijah Hurwitz, 1797.

Sefer HaBrith. Brith Milah Board of New York. Ed. by Rabbi Jacob Eskolsky (1875–1931). New York, 1915.

Sefer HaChinukh. Author unknown. Ed. by Rabbi Charles B. Chavel. Jerusalem: Mossad Harav Kook, 1953.

Sefer HaEshkhol. Rabbi Abraham ben Isaac of Narbonne (1110–1178). Tel Aviv, 1963; section 2, no. 41.

Sefer Halttur. Rabbi Isaac ben Abba Mari of Marseille (1122–1193). First printed 1873; republished Jerusalem, 1969.

Sefer HaMinhagim. Rabbi Eisik Tirna. Ed. by Shlomo J. Spitzer. Jerusalem: Mifal Torath Chakhmai Ashkenaz, 1979.

Sefer HaMitzvoth. Rabbi Moses ben Maimon (Rambam, Maimonides). Prague, 1798. Translated into English by Robert Young; Edinburgh, 1849.

Sefer HaZikhronoth. Samuel Aboab (1610–1694). New York, 1979.

Sefer Yerai'im. Rabbi Eliezer ben Sh'muail of Metz (12th cent.). Vilna, 1891–1901.

Sha'agath Aryeh. Rabbi Aryeh Leib Gunzberg (1695–1785). Frankfurt on the Oder, 1755.

Shaar HaTzi'yun. In *Mishnah B'rurah.*

Shaar Yissakhar. Chaim E. Shapira. Brooklyn, 1977.

Shaarai T'shuvah. Commentary by Rabbis Ephraim Zalman and Chaim M. Margolies. Included with *Orach Chaim.*

Shabbath. Talmudic tractate dealing with Sabbath laws.

Shakh—Sif'thai Cohen. Shabbethai ben Meir haCohen (1621–1662). In most editions of *Shulchan Arukh.*

Sheeltoth DeRav Ahai Gaon. See *Minchath Shmu'ail.*

Shekalim. Talmudic tractate dealing with annual poll tax for maintenance of the Temple in Jerusalem.

Shila. See *Sh'nai Luchoth HaBrith.*

Sh'nai Luchoth HaBrith. Rabbi Isaiah ben Abraham Horowitz (1565?–1630). Republished in New York, 1945.

Shulchan Arukh. Rabbi Yosef Caro (1488–1575). Work based on *Arbah Turim* of Rabbi Yaakov ben Asher (1270–1343) consists of four parts: *Orach Chaim, Yoreh Deah, Even HaEzer,* and *Choshen Mishpat.* First published in Venice, 1563–64; republished many times.

Shibalai HaLeket. Rabbi Tzedkia ben Avraham. Annotated edition by Shlomo Buber. Vilna, 1893.

Siddur Amram Gaon. Rav Amram ben Sheshna Gaon (d. ca. 875 C.E.) Warsaw, 1865; Jerusalem, 1971.

Siddur Avodath Yisrael. Redelheim, 1867, 1956.

Siddur Avodath Israel. New York: Hebrew Publishing Co., 1940.

Siddur Beth Yaakov. Rabbi Yaakov of Emden (1697–1776). Lemberg, 1903; New York, 1949.

Siddur HaShalaim. Jerusalem: Eshkol, no date.

Siddur Saadia Gaon (882–942). Published from MS by Israel Davidson, Simcha Assaf, and Issachar Joel. Jerusalem, 1941.

Siddur Tehillat HaShem. Prepared in accordance with text of Rabbi Shneur Zalman of Liadi (1715–1813). Translated into English by Nissen Mangel. Brooklyn, 1978.

Smag—Sefer Mitzvoth Gadol. Rabbi Moshe ben Jacob of Coucy. Kapust, 1807.

Smak—Sefer Mitzvoth Katan. Rabbi Yitzchok ben Yosef of Corbeil. Satmar, 1934.

Sod HaShem. David ben Aryeh Levy (1650–1696). Amsterdam, 1668.

Sukkah. Talmudic tractate concerned with laws relating to festival of Sukkoth.

Taamai HaMinhagim. Abraham Isaac Sperling. New York, 1944 (6th ed.).

Taanith. Talmudic tractate dealing with special communal fasts decreed in times of continued drought.

Taharoth. Talmudic tractate enunciating laws of cleanliness and uncleanliness.

Talmud. Compilation of interpretative, hermeneutic, and analytic exegesis of the Bible—the Written Law. There are two Talmuds, Babylonian (*Bavli*) and Jerusalem (*Yerushalmi*). Vilna: Romm, 1895.

Tam, Rabbainu. Rabbi Jacob ben Meir (ca. 1100–1178). A Tosafist.

Tamid. Talmudic tractate giving laws for offering of daily sacrifice.

Tanya. Rabbi Shneur Zalman of Liadi (1745–1813). Tel Aviv, 1944.

Tanya Rabathi. Rabbi Jehiel Anau. Edited by Rabbi Gedalia Felder. New York, 1975.

Taz—Turai Zahav. Rabbi David ben Samuel (1586–1667). In *Shulchan Arukh.*

Tifereth Yisrael. Commentary by Rabbi Yisrael Lipshutz (1782–1860). In many editions of Mishnah.

Torath Ha'Adam. Rabbi Moshe ben Nachaman (Ramban, Nachmanides) (1195–1270). In *Kitvai Ramban,* vol. 2, edited and annotated by Rabbi Charles B. Chavel. Jerusalem, 1967.

Torath HaBrith. Shaphtiel Davidson. Jerusalem, 1935.

Tosafoth ("additions"). Comments by a group of scholars from twelfth until fourteenth century. Published in Talmud on outer side of pages.

Tosafoth Yom Tov. Commentary by Rabbi Yom Tov Lipman Heller (1579–1654). In many editions of Mishnah.

Tosefta. Supplement to Mishnah. Rabbi Chiya and Rabbi Oshia (ca. 230 C.E.). In most editions of Talmud. Critical edition by Rabbi Saul Lieberman (1898-1983), entitled *Tosefta ki-Feshutah.*

Tur (Shulchan Arukh). Rabbi Jacob ben Asher (1269–1343). Vilna, 1900.

Turai Even on *Chagiga* and *Rosh Hashanah*. Rabbi Aryeh ben Asher (1695–1785). First published in 1781; republished in New York, 1946.

Tz'lotha D'Avraham. Rabbi Abraham Landau. Israel: Institute for Research of Jewish Liturgy, 1963.

Yad. See *Mishnah Torah*.

Yad HaKtanah. Baer ben Jacob (18th cent.). Konigsberg, 1856–59.

Yalkut Sofer. Joseph Leyb Sofer. New York, 1963.

Yam Shel Shlomo Al Kiddushin. Rabbi Solomon ben Yehiel—Maharshal (1510–1573). New York, 1952.

Yerushalmi. Jerusalem Talmud. See *Talmud*.

Yevamoth. Talmudic tractate dealing with levirate marriage and *chalitzah*.

Yoma. Talmudic tractate describing services for Day of Atonement.

Yoreh Deah. See *Shulchan Arukh*.

Yosef Umetz. Joseph Hahn (1570–1637). Frankfurt, 1928.

Y'sod Yitzchak. Rabbi Yitzchak Mezurowitz. Republished, Israel, 1967.

Zevachim. Talmudic tractate dealing with offerings brought in Temple.

Zikhron Brith L'Rishonim. Rabbi Jacob ben Gershom (12th cent.). Cracow, 1891; Jerusalem, 1970.

Zokhair David—Dinai Milah. David Zacuto Modena. Leghorn, 1837.

Zokhair HaBrith Al Hilkhoth Milah U'Pidyon Haben U'Bar Mitzvah. Asher Greenwald. Uzhgorod, 1935.

RESPONSA LITERATURE

Achiezer. Rabbi Chaim Ozer Grodzinski (1863–1940). Jerusalem, 1946.

Aimek Halakhah. Rabbi Joshua Baumol. New York, 1976.

Ain Yitzchok. Rabbi Isaac Elchanan Spektor (1817–1896). Vilna, 1888; New York, 1964.

Amudai Or. Rabbi Jehiel Heller (1814–1863). Konigsberg, 1858.

Ani Ben Pachmah. Rabbi Israel N. Kuperstock. Jerusalem, 1938.

Arugath HaBosem. Rabbi Moses Grunwald (1853–1910). Szolyva, 1912.

Atereth Chakhamim. Rabbi Baruch Teomim-Fraenkel (d. 1828).

Atzai Chaim. Rabbi Chaim Zevi Teitelbaum (1870–1926). Sighet, 1939.

Avnai Naizer. Rabbi Abraham ben Ze'ev Nahum Bornstein (1839–1910). Warsaw, 1913.

Bach, Ba'yit Chadash. Rabbi Joel Sirkes (1561–1640). Frankfurt, 1697. *Ba'yit Chadash HaChadashoth,* 1958.

Baith HaLevi. Rabbi Joseph Baer Soloveichik (1820–1892). Vilna, Warsaw, 1862–72.

Baith Ridbaz. Rabbi Jacob David Wilowsky. Jerusalem, 1904.

Baith Sh'arim. Rabbi Amram Blum (1834–1907). Munkács, 1908.

Baith Y'chezkail. Rabbi Zevi E. Michelson (1863–1942).

Baith Yitzchak. Rabbi Isaac Judah Schmelkes (d. 1905). Prezemysl, 1895.

Ben Yehudah. Rabbi Abraham Lits Rosenbaum (d. 1877). Pressburg, 1870.

Binyamin Z'aiv. Rabbi Benjamin ben Mattithiah (16th cent.). Venice, 1938.

Binyan Tzion. Rabbi Jacob Ettlinger (1798–1871). Altoona, 1867.

Birkhath R'tzai. Rabbi Tzvi Hirsch Orenstein. Lemberg, 1889.

Brith Ya'akov. Rabbi Barukh Mordecai Libschitz (1809–1885). Warsaw, 1876.

Chailek Levy. Rabbi Emanuel Pollak.

Chaishev Ha'Aifod. Rabbi Hanokh Dov Padwa. London, 1976.

Chakham Tzvi. Rabbi Zevi H. Ashkenazi (1660–1718). Amsterdam, 1712; Bnei Brak, no date.

Chatham Sofer. Rabbi Moshe Sofer (1762–1839). Vienna, 1897.

Chathan Sofer. Rabbi Samuel Ehrenfeld (1835–1883). Paks, 1911.

Chavalim BaN'imim. Rabbi Judah Loeb Graubart (1861–1937). Published, 1909.

Chavot Ya'ir. Rabbi Jair Chayim Bacharach (1638–1702). Frankfurt a.M., 1659; Lvov, 1854.

Chazon Ish, Yoreh Deah. Rabbi Avraham Yeshayahu Karelitz (1878–1953). Bnei Brak, 1973.

Chazon Nachum. Rabbi Nachom Weidenfeld. New York, 1951.

Chelkath HaSadeh. Rabbi Eliezer Chaim Deutsch (1850–1916). Published, 1899.

Chelkath Yoav. Rabbi Joab Joshua Weingarten. 3d revision, Jerusalem, 1963.

Chut HaMeshulash. Work containing writings of three rabbinic authorities. Vilna, 1882. The section by Rabbi Eliezer Yitzchak ben Hillel of Volozin discusses our theme.

Da'ath Sofer. Rabbi Akiba Sofer (Schreiber) (1878–1959). Jerusalem, 1965.

Divrai Chaim. Rabbi Chaim Halberstam (1793–1876). Lvov, 1874.

Divrai Issakhar. Rabbi Issakhar Graubart (1847–1913). Published, 1900.

Dovaiv Maisharim. Rabbi Dov Berish Weidenfeld (1859–1941). Jerusalem, 1951.

Drush Pesach, U'T'shuvah Odoth HaMetzitzah. Rabbi Jacob Emden (1697–1776). Podgorze, 1900.

D'var Avraham. Rabbi Abraham Duber Schapiro (1870–1943). Warsaw, 1905.

D'var Eliyahu. Rabbi Elijah Lerman. Warsaw, 1883.

D'var Moshe. Rabbi Moshe Teomim. Lemberg, 1864; New York, 1976.

Even Ya'akov. Rabbi Eliezer Waldenberg (b. 1917). Jerusalem, 1961.

Ezrath Yisrael. Rabbi Israel Shapiro. Warsaw, 1851.

Gur Aryai Yehudah. Rabbi Aryeh Judah Loeb Teomim (d. 1831). Published, 1827.

Ha'Elef L'kha Shlomo. Rabbi Solomon Kluger (1783–1869).

Haishiv Moshe. Rabbi Moshe Teitelbaum (1759–1841). Lvov, 1866.

Iggroth Moshe. Rabbi Moshe Feinstein (b. 1895). Israel, 1981.

Imrai Aish. Rabbi Meir Eisenstadter (1786–1852). Lvov, 1851.

Khtav Sofer. Rabbi Abraham Samuel Benjamin Sofer (1873–1938). Pressburg, 1878.

Likutai Sha'aloth U'T'shuvoth. Rabbi Moshe Sofer. New York, 1949.

Machaneh Chaim. Rabbi Chaim Sofer (1821–1886). Jerusalem, 1962.

Maharach. Rabbi Abraham ben Joseph Halevy (17th cent.). Salonika, 1897.

Maharam Alashkar. Rabbi Moses ben Isaac Alashkar (1466–1542). First printed in 1843.

Maharam Mintz. Rabbi Moshe ben Isaac Mintz (15th cent.).

Maharam Padua. Rabbi Meir Katzenellbogen (1473–1565).

Maharam Rothenberg. Rabbi Meir ben Barukh (1215–1293). Cremona, 1557.

Maishiv Davar. Rabbi Naphtali Zevi Judah Berlin (1817–1893). Warsaw, 1854.

Marchesheth. Rabbi Henach Eiges. Reprinted Jerusalem, 1968.

Mi'Ma'amakim. Rabbi Ephraim Oshry. New York, 1959.

Minchath Avraham. Rabbi Abraham Reinhald. Republished New York, 1981.

Mishk'noth Ya'akov. Rabbi Jacob ben Aaron of Karlin (1781–1844). Vilna, 1837; Jerusalem, 1959.

Mish'ptai Uziel. Rabbi Ben-Zion Ouziel (1880–1953). Tel Aviv, 1934.

M'lamaid L'Ho'il. Rabbi David Hoffman (1843–1921). Frankfurt, 1925; New York, 1954.

Neta Shurak. Rabbi Sheraha Zevi Tennenbaum (1826–1897). Munkács, 1928.

N'harai Afarsimon. Rabbi Jacob Tennenbaum (1832–1897). Republished Munkács, 1914.

Nodah B'Yehudah Tinyana. Rabbi Ezekiel Landau (1713–1793). Vilna, 1927.

Oneg Yom Tov. Rabbi Yom Tov Lipman Heilpern (1816–1879). Vilna, 1860; republished 1974.

Or HaMai'ir. Rabbi Judah M. Schapira (1887–1933). Published, 1926.

Or Zarua. Rabbi Isaac ben Moshe of Vienna.

P'air HaDor. Rambam. Lvov, 1859.

P'nai Levi. Rabbi Naphtali Joseph Freund (1861–?). Published, 1904.

P'nai Maivin. Rabbi Natanel Fried. Munkács, 1904.

Pri HaAretz. Rabbi Israel Meir ben Joseph Mizrachi (18th cent.). Salonika, 1726–34.

Pri Yitzchak. Rabbi Isaac Blaser (1840–1906). Vilna, 1880; Jerusalem, 1903.

Radbaz. Rabbi David Ibn Zimra (1479–1573). Republished Bnei Brak, 1975.

Rama. Rabbi Moshe Isserles (1520–1572). Republished Cracow, 1883.

Rashba. Rabbi Solomon ben Abraham Adret (d. 1772). Bnei Brak, 1957.

Ribash. Rabbi Isaac ben Shesheth (1326–1408). Constantinople, 1547; Jerusalem, 1972. Also known as *Yitzchak bar Shaisheth.*

Rosh. Rabbi Asher ben Yechiel (1250–1327). Published, 1950.

Shaarai Dai'a. Rabbi Chaim J.L. Litwin. Lemberg, 1877.

Shaarai Tzedek. Published by Rabbi Chaim Modai (d. 1794); includes responses of the Gaonic era. Salonika, 1797.

Shaim Aryeh. Rabbi Aryeh Balkhuver (19th cent.). Vilna, 1874; Jerusalem, 1970.

She'ilath Yavetz. Rabbi Jacob Emden. Lemberg, 1884; reprinted, 1970.

Sho'ail U'Maishiv. Rabbi Joseph Saul Nathanson (1808–1875).

Sh'vuth Yaakov. Rabbi Jacob ben Joseph Reischer (d. 1733). Lvov, 1860.

Tashbatz. Rabbi Simon ben Zemach Doran (1361–1444). 1891.

T'rumath HaDeshen. Rabbi Israel ben Pethahiah Isserlein (1390–1460). Bnei Brak, 1970.

T'shuvoth Rabbi Akiva Eger (1761–1837). Warsaw, 1875; Brooklyn, 1973.

Tuv Tam V'Daath. Rabbi Solomon Kluger (1783–1869). 3d ed. Zhitomir, 1890.

Tzafnath Panaiach. Rabbi Joseph Rosen (1858–1936). Warsaw, 1934; Jerusalem, 1978.

Tzitz Eli'ezer. Rabbi Eliezer Judah Waldenberg (b. 1917).

Tzur Yaakov. Rabbi Abraham Jacob Horowitz (1863/4–?). Jerusalem, 1955.

Ul'Ashair Amar. Rabbi Asher A. Katz. New York, 1981.

Yad Eliezer. Rabbi Eliezer Horowitz (1803–1868). Vienna, 1870.

Yad HaLevi. Rabbi Baer Bamberger (1807–1878). Jerusalem, 1964.

Yad Mai'ir. Rabbi David Frisch. Lvov, 1887.

Yad Rama. Rabbi Moses Zevi Fuchs (1843–1911). Published, 1976.

Yad Sofer. Rabbi Moshe Sofer (d. 1949). Budapest, 1948.

Yeshuoth Malko. Rabbi Israel Trunk (1820–1893). Pietrokow, 1927–39.

Zaikher Simcha. Rabbi Simon Bamberger (1832–1897). Frankfurt, 1924.

Zera Emeth. Rabbi Ishmael ben Abraham Isaac haCohen. Livorno, 1796.

Zikhron Yehudah. Rabbi Judah Grunwald (1849–1920). Published, 1922.

Zikhron Yosaif. Rabbi Joseph Steinhardt (1720–1776). Fuerth, 1773.

GENERAL

Arukh HaShulchan. Rabbi Yechiel M. Epstein (1829–1908). New York, 1960.

Benhabiles, Abdallah. *La Circumcision Chez les Muslims.* Lion et fils, 1939.

Berriman, A. E. *Historical Metrology.* New York: E. P. Dutton & Co., 1953.

Bloch, Avrohom Yechezkel. *Origin of Jewish Customs: The Jewish Child.* Brooklyn: Z. Berman Books, no date.

Book of Prayer. Ed. and trans. by Rabbi David de Sola Pool (1885–1970). New York: Union of Sephardic Congregations, 1941, 1960.

Brecher, Gideon. *Die Beschneidung der Israeliten.* Vienna, 1845.

Burns, A. R. *Money and Monetary Policy in Early Times.* New York: Alfred A. Knopf, 1927.

Chavel, Charles B. *Ramban: His Life and Teachings.* New York: Feldheim, 1960.

Dawidowicz, Lucy S. *The War Against the Jews: 1933–1945.* New York: Holt, Rinehart & Winston, 1975.

Eisenstadt, Tzvi H. "Nachmanides, His Letter About the Coin 'Shekel Israel' and Its Weight." *Talpiot* December 1949, pp. 606–621.

Emunoth V'Daioth. Saadia Gaon (882–942). Constantinople, 1562.

Fraenkel, J. *History of the Shekel,* 1956.

Ginzai Schechter. Ed. Louis Ginzberg. New York, 1928–29.

Gottlieb, Nathan. *A Jewish Child Is Born,* 1960.

———. *Welcome Home—Mother and Son: A Manual of Post-Circumcision Care.* Fair Lawn, N.J., 1969.

Gross, Chaim. *The Jewish Holidays, Customs and Traditions.* New York: Forum Gallery, 1972.

Grossman, Elliot, A. *Circumcision.* Todd and Honeywell, 1982.

Grossman, Irving. "Circumcision." Union of Orthodox Jewish Congregations. Reprinted 1982.

Guide to the Perplexed. Rabbi Moses Maimonides. Trans. and annotated by M. Friedlander. New York: Hebrew Publishing Co., no date.

Hapardes. Rabbinic Journal ed. by Rabbi Simcha Elberg, New York.

HaSiddur HaShalem. Trans. and annotated by Philip Birnbaum. New York: Hebrew Publishing Co., 1949, 1977.

Hoenig, Sidney B. Article in *Jewish Quarterly Review* 53 (1962/63): 322–324.

Ikkarim. Rabbi Yosef Albo (1357–1445). Soncino, 1485.

Jewish Communal Register of New York City: 1917–1918. New York: Kehillah, 1918.

Kaplan, Aryeh. *The Handbook of Jewish Thought.* New York: Maznaim, 1979.

Kisch, Bruno. *Scales and Weights.* New Haven: Yale University Press, 1965.

Klein, Isaac (1905–1979). *A Guide to Jewish Religious Practice.* New York: Jewish Theological Seminary, 1979.

Kohn, Samuel. *Die Geschichte der Beschneidung bei der Juden von den Altesten Zeiten bis auf die Gegenwart.* Cracow, 1903. Known also as *Oth Brith.*

Levi, Leo. *Jewish Chrononomy.* Gur Aryeh Institute, 1967.

L'Eylah. London: Office of the Chief Rabbi, Autumn 1979.

Machzor Vitry. Rabbi Simcha ben Samuel of Vitry (d. before 1105). Section 2. Ed. by Simeon Horowitz. Nurenberg, 1922.

Narkiss, M. *Matb'oth HaYehudim,* 1936.

Noam. Ed. by Rabbi Moshe S. Kasher. Torah Shelemah Institute, Jerusalem.

Oshry, Ephraim. *Churban Litah.* New York, 1952.

Otzar Dinim U'Minhagim. Rabbi Judah David Eisenstein (1854–1956). New York: Hebrew Publishing Co., 1922.

Otzar HaTefiloth. Aryeh Leib ben Shlomo Gordon and Chanokh Zundel ben Yosef. Republished New York: Sefer, 1946.

Reifenberg, Adolf. *Ancient Jewish Coins,* 1947.

Romberg, Henry C. *Bris Milah.* New York: Feldheim, 1982.

Rosen, Dov. *Shema Yisrael.* Givatayim: Peli Printing, 1972. Trans. into English from the 4th Hebrew ed. by Leonard Oschry.

Rozenzweig, Leo. *Brith Milah.* New York, 1916. This book, written in Yiddish, is an attack on the practice of *Brith Milah.*

Schauss, Hayyim. *The Lifetime of a Jew Throughout the Ages of Jewish History.* Cincinnati, 1950.

Schechter, Solomon (1847–1915). *Studies in Judaism.* Jewish Publication Society of America, 1896.

Service at a Circumcision and Service for the Redemption of the Firstborn. London: Initiation Society, 1965.

Shiurai Torah. Abraham Chaim Noe. Jerusalem, 1946.

Shiurim Shel Torah. Jacob Kanewsky. Tel Aviv, no date.

Tendler, Rabbi Moses D. "Halachah Bulletin" Subject: Mogen Circumcision Clamp. *Association of Orthodox Jewish Scientists* (no date).

Tikun Eliezer. Jesaia Jungreis, 1928.

Tucatzinsky, Jehiel. *Bain HaShemashoth.* Jerusalem: Zion Press, 1928.

Wallerstein, Edward. *Circumcision: An American Health Fallacy.* New York: Springer Publications, 1980.

BIBLIOGRAPHICAL WORKS, DICTIONARIES, AND ENCYCLOPEDIAS

Arukh HaShalaim. Rabbi Nathan ben Yechiel. Ed. by Alexander Kohut, New York, 1955.

Beth Eked Sepharim. Ch. B. Friedberg. Israel, no date.

Darkhai T'shuvah. Rabbi Tzvi Hirsch ben Shlomoh (1850–1913). Pressburg, 1893.

Encyclopaedia Britannica. Chicago, 1972.

Encyclopaedia Judaica. Israel: Keter Publishing House, 1972.

Jastrow, Marcus Mordecai (1829–1903). *Dictionary of Targumim, the Talmud Bavli and Yerushalmi and the Midrashic Literature.* First published, 1886–1903.

Jewish Encyclopedia. New York, 1901–6.

Kuntres HaT'shuvoth. Rabbi Boaz Cohen. Budapest, 1930.

Machbereth Menachem. Rabbi Menachem ibn Seruk (ca. 965 C.E.).

Me'iri. Rabbi Menachem ben Shlomoh (1249–1316).

Milon Chadosh. Avraham Even Shoshan. Jerusalem, 1956.

Milon Ivri. Yehuda Gur. Tel Aviv, 1955.

Otzar HaGeonim. Rabbi Binyamin M. Lewin (1879–1944). Haifa, 1928–42.

Otzar HaSefarim. Isaac Benjacob. Vilna: Romm, 1880.

Pachad Yitzchak. Rabbi Yitzchok Chezkiah Lampronti (1679–1756). Venice, 1750.

Sarai HaElef. Rabbi Moshe Kasher and Rabbi Dov Mandelbaum, 1959.

Steinschneider, Moritz. *Catalogus Librorum Hebraeischen in Bibliotheca Bodleiana* (1852–60).

Talmudic Encyclopedia. Jerusalem: Mossad Harav Kook, 1948–.

T'kufath HaGeonim. Rabbi Simcha Assaf (1889–1953).

T'shuvoth HaGeonim, Shaarai T'shuvah. Edited by Rabbi David Luria. Leipzig, 1858.

T'shuvoth HaGeonim, Sefer Shaarai Tzedek. Edited by Rabbi Nissin ben Chayim, 1966.

T'shuvoth HaGeonim. Avraham Eliahu Harkavy (1835–1919). Berlin, 1887.

Universal Jewish Encyclopedia. New York, 1948.
Webster's Third New International Dictionary (Unabridged). Springfield, Mass.: G. & C. Merriam Co., 1976.
Zunz, Leopold. *Zur Geschichte und Literatur,* 1845.

MEDICAL LITERATURE

Apfel, Harry. "Ritual Circumcision." *Archives of Pediatrics* 68 (1951): 427–430.
Bolande, Robert P. "Ritualistic Surgery—Circumcision and Tonsillectomy." *New England Journal of Medicine* 280, no. 11 (March 13, 1969): 591–596.
Burger, Robert, and Thomas H. Guthries. "Why Circumcision?" *Pediatrics* 54, no. 3 (September 1974).
Cansever, Gocke. "Psychological Effects of Circumcision." *British Journal of Medical Psychology* 38, no. 4 (1965): 321–331.
"Circumcision: A Balanced Report Based on Facts, Not Conjecture." *Patient Care,* July 15, 1971, pp. 56–86.
Clemente, Carmine. *Anatomy: A Regional Atlas of the Human Body.* Philadelphia: Lea & Fabiger, 1978.
"Clinical Symposia—Hypospadias and Epispadias." *Ciba* 24, no. 3 (1972).
Cohen, Eugene J., and Arthur Eidelman. *Proceedings of the Symposium on Current Concepts in Pediatrics and Urology and Their Relationship to Brith Milah.* New York: New York Board of Rabbis and Brith Milah Board of New York, 1976.
————. *Symposium on Medical Dilemmas and the Practise of Milah.* 1978.
Dodge, O. G. et al. "Circumcision and the Incidence of Carcinoma of the Penis and Cervix." *East African Medical Journal* 40 (September 1963): 440–442.
Dorland's Illustrated Medical Dictionary. 25th ed. Philadelphia: W. B. Saunders, 1974.
Gellis, Sydney S. "Circumcision." *American Journal of Diseases of Children* 132 (1978): 1168–1169.

Grossman, Elliot, and Norman Ames Posner. "Surgical Circumcision of Neonates: A History of its Development." *Obstetrics and Gynecology* 58 (1981): 241.

Hinman, Frank. Review of *Circumcision: An American Health Fallacy. Journal of the American Medical Association* 304, no. 10 (1981): 619.

Homa, Bernard. *Metzitzah*. London: Initiation Society, 1960, 1966.

Iskolsky, Jacob, ed. "Methods to be Employed by Mohelim in the Performance of Circumcision as Recommended by the Medical Members of the Milah Board of the Kehillah." 1924.

Kochen, Mosze, and Stephen McCurdy. "Circumcision and the Risk of Cancer of the Penis." *American Journal of Diseases of Children* 134 (May 1980): 484–486.

Leiter, Elliot, and Albert M. Lefkovitz. "Circumcision and Penile Carcinoma." *New York State Journal of Medicine,* August 1975, pp. 1520–1522.

Leiter, Elliot. "Circumcision—Scientist Responds to the *Times* Article." *Jewish Week,* February 11, 1979.

Maimonides, Moses (Rambam). *Pirkai Moshe.* Lemberg, 1824.

Malev, Milton. "The Jewish Orthodox Circumcision Ceremony." *Journal of the American Psychoanalytic Association,* July 1966, pp. 510–517.

Marino, Leonard J. "Counterpoint." *Nassau County Medical Center Proceedings,* Autumn 1980, pp. 103–106.

Miller, Richard L., and Donald C. Snyder. "Immediate Circumcision of the Newborn Male." *American Journal of Obstetrics and Gynecology* 65 (January 1953): 1–11.

Morgan, William K. C. "The Rape of the Phallus." *Journal of the American Medical Association* 193, no. 3 (July 19, 1965): 223–224.

Nunberg, Herman. *Problems of Bisexuality as Reflected in Circumcision."* London, 1949.

Oster, Jacob. "Further Fate of the Foreskin," *Archives of Diseases of Childhood* 43 (1968): 200–203.

Patel, Hawa. "The Problem of Routine Circumcision." *Canadian Medical Association Journal* 95 (September 10, 1966): 576–581.

Preston, E. Noel. "Whither the Foreskin." *Journal of the American Medical Association* 213, no. 11 (September 14, 1970): 1853–1858.

Preuss, Julius. *Biblical and Talmudic Medicine.* Trans. Fred Rosner. New York: Sanhedrin Press, 1978.

Pritchard, Jack A., and Paul C. MacDonald. *Williams' Obstetrics.* 16th ed., New York: Appleton-Century-Crofts, 1980.

Prucha, Zdenek S. Untitled article in *Canadian Medical Association Journal* 122 (April 5, 1980): 834.

Ravich, Abraham. "Viral Carcinogenesis in Venereally Susceptible Organs." *Cancer* 27, no. 6 (June 1971): 1493–1496.

———. *Preventing V.D. and Cancer by Circumcision.* New York: Philosophical Library, 1973.

Remondino, Peter Charles. *History of Circumcision from the Earliest Times to the Present.* Philadelphia: F. A. Davis, 1891.

Rosner, Fred. "Circumcision—Attempt at Clearer Understanding." *New York State Journal of Medicine,* November 15, 1966, pp. 2919–2922.

"Routine Circumcision Is Sharply Condemned." *Pediatrics Herald,* November 1965.

Schlosberg, Charles. "Thirty Years of Ritual Circumcision." *Clinical Pediatrics* 10, no. 4 (April 1971): 205–209.

Schlossman, Howard H. "Circumcision as Defense." *Psychoanalytic Quarterly* 5, no. 3 (July 1966): 340–356.

Schwartz, Gerhart S. Review of *Circumcision: An American Health Fallacy. Bulletin of the New York Academy of Medicine* 57, no. 9 (November 1981): 817–821.

Snowman, Jacob. *The Surgery of Ritual Circumcision.* London: Initiation Society, 1962.

Speert, Harold. "Circumcision of the Newborn." *Obstetrics and Gynecology* 2, no. 2 (August 1953): 164–172.

St. John-Hunt, D. "Correspondence." *New England Journal of Medicine* 281, no. 11 (March 13, 1969): 621–622.

Steinberg, Abraham. *Brith Milah* (Hebrew). Jerusalem: Falk Schlesinger Institute for Medical Halachic Research at Shaare Zedek Hospital, 1976.

———. Ed. *Assia*, no. 29/30 (June 1981): 21–42.

Stern, Elizabeth, and Peter A. Lachenbruch. "Circumcision Information in a Cancer Detection Center Population." *Journal of Chronic Diseases* 21 (1968): 117–124.

"The Case Against Neonatal Circumcision." *British Medical Journal*, May 5, 1979, pp. 1163–1164.

Thompson, Hugh C. et al. "Report of the Ad Hoc Task Force on Circumcision." *Pediatrics* 56, no. 4 (October 1975): 610.

Warwick, Roger, and Peter L. Williams, eds. *Gray's Anatomy*. 35th British ed., Philadelphia: W. B. Saunders Co., 1973.

Weiss, Charles. "Ritual Circumcision." *Clinical Pediatrics*, October 1962, pp. 65–72.

Whiddon, Daniel. "The Widdicombe File." *Lancet*, August 15, 1953, pp. 337–338.

Williams, William J., *Hematology*. New York: McGraw-Hill Book Co., 1977.

Wirth, John L. "Statistics on Circumcision in Canada and Australia." *American Journal of Obstetrics and Gynecology* 130 (1978): 236.

Index